ESSENTIAL
SPANISH
GRAMMAR

Seymour Resnick

TEACH YOURSELF BOOKS
Hodder and Stoughton

First published by Dover Publications Inc. 1959
Teach Yourself Books edition 1975
Eleventh impression 1987

ISBN 0 340 19494 4

Printed in Great Britain for
Hodder and Stoughton Educational,
a division of Hodder and Stoughton Ltd.,
Mill Road, Dunton Green, Sevenoaks, Kent
by Richard Clay Ltd., Bungay, Suffolk

ESSENTIAL SPANISH GRAMMAR

This book is designed specifically for those with limited learning time who want to be able to speak and understand simple, everyday Spanish. It is not a condensed outline of Spanish grammar, teaching how to construct sentences from rules and vocabulary, but a series of aids and selected points of grammar enabling the student to use Spanish phrases and words more effectively and with greater versatility. Thus, although no previous knowledge of Spanish grammar is assumed, the student should be familiar with a number of phrases and expressions such as may be found in any phrase book.

The grammatical rules and forms fundamental to the structure of the Spanish language are presented in logical sequence, and each is illustrated with useful phrases and sentences. There is a list of over 2500 words that are identical or nearly identical in form and meaning in English and Spanish, and a separate section on grammatical terms is also included.

The ideal supplement to a phrase book for the beginner, *Essential Spanish Grammar* will also be valuable as a refresher course and to those attending Spanish conversation classes.

TEACH YOURSELF BOOKS

Contents

Introduction

Essential Spanish Grammar assumes that you will be spending a limited number of hours studying Spanish grammar and that your limited objective is simple everyday communication. It is offered not as a condensed outline of all aspects of the grammar, but as a series of aids which will enable you to use more effectively and with greater versatility phrases and vocabulary that you have previously learned. It will familiarize you with the more common structure and patterns of the language and give you a selected number of the most useful rules and paradigms.

If you have studied Spanish in a conventional manner, you will probably understand everything in *Essential Spanish Grammar*, which could then serve as a refresher even though it takes a different approach from conventional grammars. You may want to glance through the book and then pay attention to those areas in which you are weak.

But if this is your first introduction to Spanish grammar the following suggestions will be helpful.

1. Don't approach this book until you have mastered many useful phrases and expressions such as you will find in any good phrase book. Everything will be more comprehensible and usable after you have achieved some simple, working knowledge of the language. The purpose of this book is to enable you to achieve greater fluency with the phrase approach, not to teach you to construct sentences from rules and vocabulary.

2. Start at the beginning of this book and read through it. Look up unfamiliar or confusing grammatical terms in the short glossary in the rear. Don't be concerned if sections are not immediately clear to you. On a second or third reading they will make better sense. What may appear discouragingly difficult at first will become understandable as your studies progress. As you use the language and hear it spoken, many aspects of Spanish grammar will begin to form recognizable patterns. If *Essential Spanish Grammar* does nothing more than acquaint you with some of the structure and nature of this grammar it will be helpful to you in developing your vocabulary, phrases and generally improving your comprehension.

3. Go back to this book periodically. Sections which seem difficult or of doubtful benefit to you now may prove extremely helpful later on.

4. For the most part, *Essential Spanish Grammar* is presented in a logical order, especially for the major divisions of grammar, and you will do best if you follow its sequence in your studies. However, the author is aware that some students learn best when they study to answer their immediate questions and needs (e.g. how to form the comparative; the declension of the verb *to be*, etc.). If you prefer to work in this manner, study entire sections rather than isolated parts of sections:

5. Examples are given for every rule. You may find it helpful to memorize the examples. If you learn every example given in this supplement and its literal translation you will have met the most basic problems of Spanish grammar and examples for their solution.

There are many ways to express the same thought. Languages have different constructions for expressing the same idea; some simple, others difficult. An elusive verb conjugation may well be a more sophisticated form of expression and one you may ultimately wish to master; but during your first experiments in communication you can achieve your aim by using a simple form, which will still result in perfectly acceptable grammar. Try to work out easy ways for expressing complex ideas rather than translating ideas word for word. Throughout this grammar you'll find helpful hints on how to avoid difficult constructions.

As you begin to speak Spanish you will be your own best judge of the areas in which you need help in grammatical construction. If there's no one with whom to practise, speak mentally to yourself. In the course of a day, see how many of the simple thoughts you've expressed in English can be stated in some manner in Spanish. This kind of experimental self-testing will give direction to your study of grammar. Remember that you are studying this course in Spanish not to pass an examination or receive a certificate, but to communicate with others on a simple but useful level. *Essential Spanish Grammar* is not the equivalent of a formal course at a university. Although it could serve as a supplement to a formal course, its primary aim is to help the adult study on his own. Indeed, no self study or academic course could ever be offered that is ideally suited to every potential student. You must therefore rely on and be guided by your own rate of learning, your own requirements and interests.

If this grammar or any other grammar tends to inhibit your use of the language you may have learned through a simple phrase approach as taught in some schools, curtail your study of grammar until you really feel it will assist rather than hinder your speaking. Your objective is speaking and you *can* learn to speak a language without formal grammatical training. The fundamental purpose of *Essential Spanish Grammar* is to enable you to learn more rapidly and eliminate hit-or-miss memorization. For those who are at home with a more systematic approach, grammar will enable them to learn more quickly.

The primary purpose of this grammar is not to teach you perfect Spanish but to communicate and make yourself understood. If its goal is achieved you will be speaking Spanish and making mistakes rather than maintaining a discreet silence. In most cases it is better to speak and make mistakes than not to speak at all. *Se aprende a hablar, hablando.* One learns to speak by speaking.

Abbreviations used in *Essential Spanish Grammar*

M.	Masculine
F.	Feminine
SING.	Singular
PL.	Plural
LIT.	Literally
Ud., Vd.	Usted
Uds., Vds.	Ustedes

Italics and bold faces have been used in this grammar to make important points more obvious to you. These diversities in type do not mean that Spanish is written or printed in varying type faces. Nor do they mean that special stress or accent is given to syllables or words. They are used purely as a typographical convenience, to make you remember endings or to call your attention to key words.

Vocabulary and Vocabulary Building

The following suggestions may be helpful to you in building your vocabulary:

1. Study words and word lists that answer real and preferably immediate personal needs. If you are planning to travel in the near future your needs are clear and any good phrase book gives you the material you will want. Select material according to your personal interests and needs. If you don't plan to drive, don't spend time studying parts of the car. If you like foreign foods, study the appropriate part of your phrase book. Even if you do not plan to travel in the near future, you will probably learn more quickly by imagining yourself in a travel or real-life situation.

2. Use the mnemonic technique of association. For the most part a phrase book gives you associated word lists. If you continue to build your vocabulary by memorization don't use a dictionary for this purpose. Select grammars or books that have lists of associated words.

3. Study the specialized vocabulary of your profession, business or hobby. If you are interested in real estate learn the many terms associated with property, buying, selling, leasing, etc. An interest in mathematics should lead you to a wide vocabulary in this science. Words in your speciality will be learned quickly and a surprising amount will be applicable or transferable to other areas. Although these specialized vocabularies are not readily available in book literature, an active interest and a good dictionary are all you really need.

Word Order

Word order in Spanish is frequently the same as in English. Since many words in Spanish are obviously related in appearance and derivation to English words, it is often a simple matter to understand a Spanish sentence if you know only a minimum of grammar.*

Madrid está en el centro de la península ibérica.
Madrid is in the centre of the Iberian peninsula.

Los turistas generalmente visitan los puntos de interés.
The tourists generally visit the points of interest.

* If you are not sure about the terms and concepts used in grammar we suggest that you read the glossary of grammatical terms at the end of this book before you begin your study of Spanish.

How to Turn a Positive Sentence into a Negative Sentence

You can convert any of the sentences in your phrase book or records into negative sentences by simply placing *no* (which means both *no* and *not*) before the verb of the sentence.

Esta ciudad *no* es muy grande.
This city is *not* very large.

Yo *no* hablo muy bien.
I do *not* speak very well.

How to Form Questions

There are three very easy ways to turn ordinary statements into questions. You can take almost any sentence out of your phrase book, and by treating it in one of these three ways make it a question.

1. It is possible to form a question in Spanish without changing the original word order at all, simply by raising your voice. We sometimes do this in English, too. In written Spanish you are warned that a question is coming by an inverted question mark at the beginning of the sentence.

¿Usted habla inglés?
Do you speak English?

2. We may also form questions by placing the predicate in front of the subject of the sentence. This same construction is used in English.

¿Es importante el primer capítulo?
Is the first chapter important?

¿Habla usted inglés?
Do you speak English?

3. A third common way of making an ordinary statement into a question is by adding *¿no?* or *¿verdad?* or *¿no es verdad?* to the end of the statement. These correspond to the English phrases *Isn't it? Don't you? Aren't you? Didn't they?* etc.

Usted habla inglés, *¿verdad?*
You speak English, *don't you?*

El primer capítulo es importante, *¿no?*
The first chapter is important, *isn't it?*

Study the following sentences, which contain the most important interrogative words. For the written language, note that all these interrogative words bear a written accent.

¿Qué desea usted?
What do you wish?

¿Cómo puedo ir al centro?
How can I go to the centre of the town?

¿Cuándo sale el último tren?
When does the last train leave?

¿Dónde está la estación?
Where is the station?

¿Cuál prefiere usted?
Which one do you prefer?

¿Cuánto cuesta?
How much does it cost?

¿Cuántos necesita usted?
How many do you need?

¿Por qué está usted tan cansado?
Why are you so tired?

¿De quién es este reloj?
Whose watch is this?

¿Quién sabe?
Who knows?

Nouns

All nouns in Spanish are either masculine or feminine.
Almost all nouns ending in *-o* are masculine, while those
ending in *-a*, or *-d*, or *-ción* are usually feminine. (Two important exceptions are *la mano, the hand,* and *el día, the day,*
which are, respectively, feminine and masculine.) With other
endings you have to learn the gender when you learn the
noun. The easiest way of doing this is by learning the word
the along with the noun. The masculine singular form is *el,*
masculine plural is *los*; feminine singular is *la,* feminine
plural is *las.*

To form the plural of nouns just add *-s* to words ending
with a vowel, and *-es* to words ending with a consonant.
Study the following examples:

el profesor	the teacher	la mujer	the woman
los profesor*es*	the teachers	las mujer*es*	the women
el libro	the book	la camisa	the shirt
los libro*s*	the books	las camis*as*	the shirts
el guante	the glove	la lección	the lesson
los guante*s*	the gloves	las leccion*es*	the lessons

Many masculine nouns ending in *-o,* referring to persons
have a feminine equivalent in *-a.*

el hij*o*	the son	el amig*o*	the friend (M.)
la hij*a*	the daughter	la amig*a*	the friend (F.)

17

| el chico | the boy | el hermano | the brother |
| la chica | the girl | la hermana | the sister |

The word for *a* or *an* is *un*, masculine, and *una*, feminine.

| *un* traje | a suit | *una* playa | a beach |
| *un* edificio | a building | *una* luz | a light |

Adjectives

In Spanish adjectives have to agree in number and gender with the nouns they accompany. We have nothing comparable to this in English. In most cases, also contrary to English usage, adjectives follow their nouns.

If the masculine form of the adjective ends in -o, the feminine form ends in -a, and the plurals are -os and -as respectively.

el señor simpático	the charming gentleman
la señora simpática	the charming lady
los señores simpáticos	the charming gentlemen
las señoras simpáticas	the charming ladies

If the masculine singular of the adjective ends in -e the feminine singular is the same as the masculine, and the plural for both genders is formed by adding -s.

un país importante	an important country
una familia importante	an important family
países importantes	important countries
familias importantes	important families

If the masculine adjectival form ends in a consonant there is no change for the feminine singular, and we form the plural of both genders by adding -es.

un juego difícil	a difficult game
una lengua difícil	a difficult language
juegos difíciles	difficult games
lenguas difíciles	difficult languages

Adverbs

In English we often form adverbs by adding *-ly* to an adjective, as in *clear, clearly, new, newly*. In Spanish many adverbs are formed similarly by adding *-mente* to the feminine form of the adjective.

absolut*o*	absolute
absoluta*mente*	absolutely
clar*o*	clear
clara*mente*	clearly
rápid*o*	rapid
rápida*mente*	rapidly

Usted debe hablar más claramente.
You ought to speak more clearly.

Two common adverbs that do not end in *-mente* are: *despacio, slowly* and *demasiado, too much*.

Expressing Possession

The English way of expressing possession by apostrophe
s, *teacher's book*, is not used in Spanish. Instead, forms
comparable to the other English style, *the book of the teacher*,
are used.

el palacio *del* rey	the palace *of the king* (the king'*s* palace)
las casas *de* mi padre	the houses *of* my father (my father'*s* houses)

Note that in Spanish the definite article can often be used
to indicate possession with parts of the body and articles of
clothing.

Déme *la* mano.	Give me your hand.
Me quité *los* zapatos.	I took off my shoes.

The possessive adjectives are as follows:

SING.	PL.	
mi	mis	my
su	sus	your (SING.), his, her, its
nuestro (M.)	nuestros (M.)	our
nuestra (F.)	nuestras (F.)	
su	sus	your (PL.), their

Observe that these words, like other adjectives, have to
agree in number and gender with the noun that they
accompany.

Necesito *mi* pasaporte.
I need my passport.

¿Dónde están nuestra*s* maleta*s*?
Where are our valises?

¿Cuál es *su* dirección?
What is your address?

After the verb *ser*, *to be*, we use special forms to express ownership.

SING.	PL.	
mío (M.),	míos	mine
mía (F.)	mías	,,
suyo (M.), suya (F.)	suyos, suyas	yours, his, her, its
nuestro (M.)	nuestros,	ours
nuestra (F.)	nuestras	,,
suyo (M.), suya (F.)	suyos, suyas	yours, theirs

These forms, too, must agree with the nouns they accompany, even though the noun is separated from them by forms of the verb, *to be*.

Este coch*e* no es *mio*.
This car isn't mine.

Los papel*es* blancos son nuestr*os*.
The white papers are ours.

Demonstrative Adjectives and Pronouns

This and *that*, *these* and *those* are translated as follows:

este hombre	this man	*esta* mujer	this woman
estos hombres	these men	*estas* mujeres	these women
ese hombre	that man	*esa* mujer	that woman
esos hombres	those men	*esas* mujeres	those women

That may also be translated as *aquel* (M.), *aquella* (F.), *aquellos* (M.PL.), *aquellas* (F.PL.), when it refers to something in the distance.

> Mire usted *aquellas* montañas.
> Look at *those* mountains.

The neuter demonstrative pronouns are *esto* and *eso* for *this* and *that* respectively.

> ¿Qué es *esto*?   What is *this*?
> *Eso* es.   *That* is it; *that* is right.

If you are referring to specific objects, and are differentiating between two or more things in a series, the adjectives above serve as pronouns. They then take a written accent (which does not affect pronunciation).

> No quiero *éste*; déme *ése*, por favor.
> I don't want *this one*; give me *that one*, please.

> ¿Cuáles prefiere usted, *éstos* o *aquéllos*?
> Which ones do you prefer, *these* or *those*?

Comparisons

In English we make comparative forms by adding *-er* to the end of some adjectives, and by placing *more* in front of adverbs, nouns and other adjectives. (Example: John is richer and more influential than Peter.) In Spanish you form such comparatives and superlatives by placing the word *más* (*more*) before the noun, adjective or adverb concerned. The word *than* in such cases is translated by *que*.

Mi prima tiene *más* discos *que* nadie.
My cousin has *more* records *than* anyone.

Este paquete es *más* ligero *que* el suyo.
This package is light*er than* yours.

Son *más* inteligentes *que* sus vecinos.
They are *more* intelligent *than* their neighbours.

Repítalo *más* despacio.
Repeat it *more* slowly.

Los cubanos hablan *más* rápidamente *que* los mexicanos.
Cubans speak *more* rapidly *than* Mexicans.

Usted pronuncia *mejor quo* yo.
You pronounce *better than* I.

Es la chica *más hermosa* del pueblo.
She is the *prettiest* girl in town.

Most adjectives and adverbs form their comparatives regularly, as above. A noteworthy exception, however, is *bueno* (*good*), which has *mejor* (*better*) as its comparative. *Mejor* is also the comparative for the adverb *bien* (*well*).

Comparisons of equality (*as . . . as*) are translated *tan . . . como* with adjectives and adverbs, and *tanto, -a, -os, -as . . . como* with nouns.

Soy *tan* alto *como* mi hermano.
I am *as* tall *as* my brother.

Hable *tan* despacio *como* yo.
Speak *as* slowly *as* I do.

No tengo *tanto* dinero *como* ustedes.
I haven't got *as* much money *as* you.

Nadie tiene *tantas* tarjetas *como* yo.
No one has *as* many cards *as* I have.

Pronouns

In Spanish, as in English, pronouns have different forms according to their use or position in a sentence.

The simplest forms, those which are used as subjects for sentences, are as follow:

yo	I	nosotros	we
usted	you (SING.)	ustedes	you (PL.)
él	he	ellos	they (M.)
ella	she	ellas	they (F.)

Direct and Indirect Object Pronouns

The object pronouns (*me, you, him, her, it, us, them*) are either direct (He takes *it*) or indirect (He gives *me* the book, or, He gives the book to *me*). In Spanish the *object* pronouns are as follows:

	Indirect		*Direct*
me	(to) me	me	me
		le	you, him
le	(to) you, him, her, it	lo	him, it (M.)
		la	you, her, it (F.)
nos	(to) us	nos	us
les	(to) you, them	los	them, you (M.)
		las	them, you (F.)

Their position is before the verb. However, with the infinitive or an affirmative command they are suffixed to the end of the verb. Study the following sentences:

Nos dieron el dinero.
They gave *us* the money.

Le expliqué el problema.
I explained the problem *to him*.

No *la* veo ahora, pero *le* hablé hace media hora.
I don't see *her* now, but I spoke *to her* half an hour ago.

Quiero escuchar*los*.
I want to listen to *them*.

Díga*me* le verdad.
Tell *me* the truth.

No *me* moleste ahora.
Don't bother *me* now.

When there are two object pronouns the indirect object precedes the direct object.

Me lo dice.	He tells it *to me*.
Díga*me*lo.	Tell it *to me*.

If both object pronouns, however, are third person the indirect pronoun becomes *se* instead of *le* or *les*.

Se lo dice.	He tells it *to him* (*her*, *you*, *them*).

To avoid this difficult object construction we suggest that you express yourself differently. By using the preposition *a* (*to*) and the prepositional pronouns given in the following section, you can express the same thought much more easily.

Lo dice *a él*.	He tells it *to him*.
Lo dice *a ella*.	He tells it *to her*.
Lo dice *a usted*.	He tells it *to you*.
Lo dice *a ellos*.	He tells it *to them*.

Prepositional Forms of the Personal Pronouns

The pronoun forms used after prepositions (*for, with, against, to, among,* etc.) are the same as the subject pronouns in Spanish (*yo, usted, él, ella, nosotros, ustedes, ellos, ellas*), except for the first person singular, which is *mí*, not *yo.* Study the following:

para *mí*	for *me*
sin *usted*	without *you*
con *él**	with *him*
a *ella*	to *her*
cerca de *nosotros*	near *us*
delante de *ustedes*	in front of *you*
entre *ellos*	among *them*
por *ellas*	by *them*

Table of Personal Pronouns

To help review the pronouns presented in the last few sections, the following table of personal pronouns will be a useful reference. For the sake of completeness we include the familiar singular and familiar plural forms (in parentheses), used in addressing children, close friends and relatives, and animals. These forms should be avoided by the beginner or traveller. Use *usted* for *you* (SING.) and *ustedes* for *you* (PL.).

The last column, reflexive pronoun objects, will be taken up when you study the reflexive verb on page 52.

Subject	Preposi- tional	Indirect Object	Direct Object	Reflexive Object
yo	mí	me	me	me
(tú)	(ti)	(te)	(te)	(te)

* Note that *with me* is *conmigo.*

Subject	Preposi-tional	Indirect Object	Direct Object	Reflexive Object
él	él	le	le, lo	se
ella	ella	le	la	se
usted	usted	le	le, la	se
nosotros	nosotros	nos	nos	nos
(vosotros)	(vosotros)	(os)	(os)	(os)
ellos	ellos	les	los	se
ellas	ellas	les	las	se
ustedes	ustedes	les	los, las	se

Note the great similarity between the subject and pre-positional forms, and the closeness of indirect, direct and reflexive objects.

Negatives

As pointed out on page 14, we can make sentences negative by placing *no* before the verb. Other important negatives are *nunca, never*; *nada, nothing*; *nadie, nobody*. *Nunca* may either precede the verb in place of *no*, or it may follow the verb in addition to *no*.

Nunca he estado aquí.	I've *never* been here.
No he estado aquí *nunca*.	I've *never* been here.

This combination of *no*, verb and negative pronoun or adverb is called the double negative construction. *Nada* usually takes this construction.

No veo nada.	I don't see anything ("nothing").

Nadie generally precedes the verb when it is the subject and follows the verb when it is the object.

Nadie puede hacer eso.	*Nobody* can do that.
No ví a *nadie*.	I did *not* see *anyone*.

The Contractions *al* and *del*

There are only two contractions in the Spanish language. *A* and *el* become *al,* and *de* and *el* become *del.*

Mandé un telegrama *al* presidente *del* país.
I sent a telegram *to the* president *of the* country.

Vamos *al* mercado *del* pueblo.
Let's go *to the* town market.

Personal *a*

A peculiarity of Spanish is that the preposition *a* is placed before a direct object (except of the verb 'tener'), if the object is a definite person.

¿Ha visto Vd. *a* mi primo?
Have you seen my cousin?

Busco *al* gerente.
I am looking for the manager.

Vamos a visitar *a* los señores García.
Let's visit Mr. and Mrs. García.

The Word *que*

In English we frequently omit the word *that* when it is a conjunction. (*I think that he will come*, or *I think he will come*.) In Spanish the conjunction *que* must be expressed.

Creo *que* vendrá.
I think (*that*) he will come.

¿Sabe Vd. *que* no están casados?
Do you know (*that*) they are not married?

In addition to being a conjunction, *que* is also the most important relative pronoun (*who, which, that, whom*), since it may refer to either persons or things, and may be used as either subject or object. The following sentences illustrate its uses:

No encuentro el diccionario *que* compré ayer.
I can't find the dictionary (*which*) I bought yesterday.

El hombre *que* hizo eso ya no vive aquí.
The man *who* did that no longer lives here.

Aquí tiene usted un abrigo *que* no cuesta mucho.
Here is a coat *that* does not cost much.

Es el mismo mozo *que* tuvimos ayer.
He's the same waiter (*that*) we had yesterday.

Verbs

The Present Tense

In English verbs are rather simple. Very few endings are added, and these are relatively uniform (I sing, he sing*s*, I take, he take*s*). In Spanish more endings are used, and these tell you the person and number of the subject. There are three such sets of endings or conjugations; and each verb belongs to one. You can tell the conjugation of a verb by looking at its infinitive (the form which corresponds to the English *to walk, to have*, etc.). Memorize the following tables.

First conjugation   Infinitive ending *-ar*

	hablar (to speak)
(yo) habl*o*	I speak, am speaking
(usted) habl*a*	you (SING.) speak, are speaking
(él, ella) habl*a*	he, she, it speaks, is speaking
(nosotros) habl*amos*	we speak, are speaking
(ustedes) habl*an*	you (PL.) speak, are speaking
(ellos, ellas) habl*an*	they speak, are speaking

Second conjugation   Infinitive ending *-er*

	comer (to eat)
(yo) com*o*	I eat, am eating
(usted) com*e*	you (SING.) eat, are eating
(él, ella) com*e*	he, she, it eats, is eating
(nosotros) com*emos*	we eat, are eating
(ustedes) com*en*	you (PL.) eat, are eating
(ellos, ellas) com*en*	they eat, are eating

35

Third conjugation   Infinitive ending -*ir*

escribir (to write)

(yo) escrib*o*	I write, am writing
(usted) escrib*e*	you (SING.) write, are writing
(él, ella) escrib*e*	he, she, it writes, is writing
(nosotros) escrib*imos*	we write, are writing
(ustedes) escrib*en*	you (PL.) write, are writing
(ellos, ellas) escrib*en*	they write, are writing

Several points should be noted:

1. The subject pronouns *yo, él, ella, nosotros, ellos, ellas* are often omitted. The subject pronouns *usted* and *ustedes, you,* however, are usually used.

2. The first person singular ending for all verbs (except for a few irregular instances to be given later) is -*o*.

3. The *usted* (abbreviated *Ud.* or *Vd.*) form of the verb is the same as the *él* or *ella* form, and the *ustedes* (abbreviated *Uds.* or *Vds.*) form is the same as the *ellos* or *ellas* form. In the following verb tables, therefore, only four forms will be given, instead of six.

4. The third person plural forms (*they . . .*) are formed by adding -*n* to the third person singular forms (*he . . .*), *habla, hablan; come, comen.*

5. The second and third conjugation endings are the same except for the first person plural, -*emos*, -*imos*, respectively.

6. The first person plural ending always has the characteristic vowel of the infinitive -*amos*, -*emos*, -*imos*.

7. The same form in Spanish can be translated as both simple present in English (*I speak*) and the progressive present (*I am speaking*).

8. Besides *usted* and *ustedes* there is another way of saying *you* in Spanish. A familiar singular form *tú* is used to address close friends, relatives, children and animals. Its verb forms end in *-s* (*hablas, you speak, comes, you eat,* and *escribes, you write*). The plural familar form is *vosotros,* and its verb forms are *habláis, you speak, coméis, you eat,* and *escribís, you write.* You will probably have no opportunity to use these forms, and should avoid them; we mention them only so that you will recognize them if you hear them. Concentrate instead on the polite forms *usted* and *ustedes.*

Irregular Verbs

There are a few irregular verbs which are very frequently used, and which must be learned. Here is the present tense of the most important of these verbs. To simplify learning, verb conjugations are presented in the following pattern: the first person singular, second and third person singular; the first person plural, second and third person plural.

Example:

decir (to say)

digo	I say
dice	you (SING.) say; he says, she says
decimos	we say
dicen	you (PL.) say; they say

decir	to say, tell	digo, dice, decimos, dicen
hacer	to do, make	hago, hace, hacemos, hacen
oír	to hear	oigo, oye, oímos, oyen
poner	to put, place	pongo, pone, ponemos, ponen
salir	to leave, go out	salgo, sale, salimos, salen
tener	to have	tengo, tiene, tenemos, tienen
traer	to bring	traigo, trae, traemos, traen

venir	to come	vengo, viene, venimos, vienen
dar	to give	doy, da, damos, dan
ir	to go	voy, va, vamos, van
saber	to know	sé, sabe, sabemos, saben
ver	to see	veo, ve, vemos, ven

Stem-changing Verbs

Some verbs change their stems in the present tense of all persons except the first plural. After dropping the infinitive ending *-ar*, *-er*, *-ir*, the *e* of the last syllable changes to *ie*, and an *o* in the last syllable changes to *ue*. These changes affect all three conjugations. Some verbs of the third conjugation only, *-ir*, may have a change of *e* to *i*. Study the following examples.

pensar (ie)	to think	pienso, piensa, pensamos, piensan
querer (ie)	to want, like, love	quiero, quiere, queremos, quieren
contar (ue)	to count	cuento, cuenta, contamos, cuentan
poder (ue)	to be able	puedo, puede, podemos, pueden
pedir (i)	to ask (for)	pido, pide, pedimos, piden

Other common verbs of this type are given here. The change is indicated in parentheses.

cerrar (ie)	to close	cierro, cierra, cerramos, cierran
comenzar (ie)	to begin	comienzo, comienza, comenzamos, comienzan
costar (ue)	to cost	cuesto, cuesta, costamos, cuestan
despertar (ie)	to awaken	despierto, despierta, despertamos, despiertan

dormir (ue)	to sleep	duermo, duerme, dormimos, duermen
empezar (ie)	to begin	empiezo, empieza, empezamos, empiezan
encontrar (ue)	to find, meet	encuentro, encuentra, encontramos, encuentran
entender (ie)	to understand	entiendo, entiende, entendemos, entienden
jugar (ue)	to play	juego, juega, jugamos, juegan
morir (ue)	to die	muero, muere, morimos, mueren
mostrar (ue)	to show	muestro, muestra, mostramos, muestran
perder (ie)	to lose	pierdo, pierde, perdemos, pierden
preferir (ie)	to prefer	prefiero, prefiere, preferimos, prefieren
repetir (i)	to repeat	repito, repite, repetimos, repiten
seguir (i)	to follow	sigo, sigue, seguimos, siguen
sentar (ie)	to seat	siento, sienta, sentamos, sientan
sentir (ie)	to regret, feel	siento, siente, sentimos, sienten
servir (i)	to serve	sirvo, sirve, servimos, sirven
vestir (i)	to dress	visto, viste, vestimos, visten
volar (ue)	to fly	vuelo, vuela, volamos, vuelan
volver (ue)	to return	vuelvo, vuelve, volvemos, vuelven

The Verbs *Ser* and *Estar*

In English, although we do not realize it when we speak, we express many different ideas with the verb *to be*. *Are*, for example, can mean *are located* (*Granada and Barcelona are in Spain*.), *equal* (*Two and two are four*.), or *have the characteristic of being* (*Apples are red*.). Spanish, however, uses two different verbs (*estar* and *ser*) for the ideas we express with *to be*. *Estar* is used to express location and condition; condition includes adjectives that describe a state of emotion or health (*triste*, *sad*; *contento*, *glad*; *enfermo*, *sick*; *cansado*, *tired*, etc.). *Ser* is used in most other cases, especially to indicate a permanent quality. Memorize the irregular present tense of these important verbs and study the following sentences.

estar	ser	to be
estoy	soy	I am
está	es	you are (SING.); he, she, it is
estamos	somos	we are
están	son	you are (PL.), they are

The following sentences illustrate condition or location. *Estar* is used.

> Madrid está en el centro geográfico de la península ibérica.
>
> Madrid is in the geographic centre of the Iberian peninsula. (location)

> La catedral no está lejos de aquí.
>
> The cathedral is not far from here. (location)

> ¿Dónde están mis anteojos?
>
> Where are my spectacles? (location)

> ¿Cómo están ustedes?
>
> How are you? (condition)

Estamos un poquito cansados.
We are a little tired. (condition)

¿Por qué está usted tan triste hoy?
Why are you so sad today? (condition)

The following sentences are not statements of condition
or location, but of essence, and *ser* is therefore used.

Somos turistas de los Estados Unidos.
We are tourists from the United States.

Madrid es la capital de España.
Madrid is the capital of Spain.

Nuestro guía es muy bueno.
Our guide is very good.

Su novia no es rica, pero es muy bella.
His girl friend is not rich, but she is very beautiful.

¿Quién es usted? Soy el señor Miller.
Who are you? I am Mr. Miller.

Estar is also used to form the progressive tense, which
corresponds to the English *to be* plus a present participle
(*I am walking, you are reading,* etc.). In Spanish the present
participle is formed by dropping the infinitive ending *-ar,*
-er, -ir, and adding *-ando* to the first conjugation, and *-iendo*
to the second and third conjugations.

comprar	comprando	buying
llover	lloviendo	raining
sufrir	sufriendo	suffering

The progressive tense is more vivid than the simple
present, but the simple present can always be used in Spanish.

Estoy escribiendo una carta a mi familia *or, Escribo* una
  carta a mi familia.
I am writing a letter to my family.

Estamos visitando muchos lugares hermosos *or,*
    Visitamos muchos lugares hermosos.
We are visiting many beautiful places.

¿Qué *está* usted *haciendo*? *or,* ¿Qué *hace* usted?
What *are* you *doing*?

The Command Form

To obtain the command form of almost any verb we take
the first person singular of the present tense, drop the -*o*
and add the following endings: -*ar* verbs add -*e* (SING.),
and -*en* (PL.), while -*er* and -*ir* verbs add -*a* (SING.) and -*an*
(PL.). For example, *to come* is *venir*, *I come* is *vengo* (see
page 38); therefore the command *Come!* is ¡*Venga (Vd.)!*
in the singular and ¡*Vengan (Vds.)!* in the plural. Notice
that the pronoun, when it is used, is placed after the verb.

bajar	to come down	baje (Vd.), bajen (Vds.)
pagar	to pay	pague (Vd.), paguen * (Vds.)
recordar	to remember	recuerde (Vd.), recuerden (Vds.)
comer	to eat	coma (Vd.), coman (Vds.)
escribir	to write	escriba (Vd.), escriban (Vds.)
servir	to serve	sirva (Vd.), sirvan (Vds.)
volver	to return	vuelva (Vd.), vuelvan (Vds.)
decir	to say, tell	diga (Vd.), digan (Vds.)

The command is usually softened and rendered more
polite by adding *por favor*, *please*.

Abra Vd. la ventana, por favor.
Please open the window.

Siéntese, por favor.
Please sit down.

---

* Since *g* before *e* or *i* has the sound of a harsh *h*, *u* must be inserted
in these forms to keep the hard *g* sound of the infinitive.

Tráigame otro vaso, por favor.
Please bring me another glass.

Another way of expressing a command is to use the phrase *Hágame Vd. el favor de* with the infinitive, *Do me the favour of . . .*

Hágame Vd. el favor de abrir la ventana.
Please open the window.

Hágame Vd. el favor de traducir esta frase.
Please translate this sentence.

The verb *ir, to go*, has an irregular command: *vaya Vd.* and *vayan Vds.*

Vaya con Dios.   Go with God.*

The first person plural command form (*let's*, with the infinitive) is best translated by *vamos a* with the infinitive. *Vamos* alone means *let us go*.

Vamos al cine esta noche.	Let's go to the cinema tonight.
Vamos a ver.	Let's see.
Vamos a cantar.	Let's sing.
Vamos a jugar.	Let's play.

The Past Tense

Spanish, like English, has several ways of expressing a past event. The past tense which will be most useful is the preterite, which corresponds to the English simple past (*I went, I left, I bought*, etc.). It is formed by dropping the infinitive ending and adding *-é, -ó, -amos, -aron* to the stem of the first conjugation, and *-í, -ió, -imos, -ieron* to the stems of the second and third conjugations.

* Often used as a way of saying *good-bye*.

First conjugation   *-ar*

	comprar (to buy)
compré	I bought
compró	you (SING.), he, she, it bought
compramos	we bought
compraron	you (PL.), they bought

Second conjugation   *-er*

	perder (to lose)
perdí	I lost
perdió	you, he, she, it lost
perdimos	we lost
perdieron	you, they lost

Third conjugation   *-ir*

	salir (to leave)
salí	I left
salió	you, he, she, it left
salimos	we left
salieron	you, they left

There are some important verbs which are irregular in the preterite. These should be memorized.

dar	to give	dí, dió, dimos, dieron
decir	to say, tell	dije, dijo, dijimos, dijeron
estar	to be	estuve, estuvo, estuvimos, estuvieron
hacer	to do, make	hice, hizo, hicimos, hicieron
ir	to go	fuí, fué, fuimos, fueron
ser	to be	fuí, fué, fuimos, fueron
poner	to put, place	puse, puso, pusimos, pusieron
tener	to have	tuve, tuvo, tuvimos, tuvieron
traer	to bring	traje, trajo, trajimos, trajeron
venir	to come	vine, vino, vinimos, vinieron

Observe that the verbs *ir* and *ser* have the same preterite forms.

Study the following sentences.

> *Llegaron* ayer y *fueron* immediatamente al consulado americano.
>
> *They arrived* yesterday and *went* to the American consulate immediately.

> ¿Qué *hizo* usted anoche?
> What *did* you *do* last night?

> *Llamé* a Juan y *fuimos* juntos al teatro.
> *I called* John and *we went* to the theatre together.

The Imperfect Tense

The imperfect tense describes what was happening or what used to happen. It is formed by dropping the infinitive ending and adding *-aba, -aba, -ábamos, -aban* to the stem of first conjugation verbs, and *-ía, -ía, -íamos, -ían* to the stems of second and third conjugation verbs.

First conjugation   *-ar*

pagar (to pay)

pag*aba*	I paid, used to pay, was paying
pag*aba*	you, he, she, it paid, used to pay, was paying, were paying
pag*ábamos*	we paid, used to pay, were paying
pag*aban*	you, they, paid, used to pay, were paying

Second conjugation   *-er*

creer (to believe)

cre*ía*	I believed, used to believe
cre*ía*	you, he, she, it believed, used to believe
cre*íamos*	we believed, used to believe
cre*ían*	they, you believed, used to believe

Third conjugation   *-ir*

vivir (to live)

viv*ía*	I lived, used to live, was living
viv*ía*	you, he, she, it lived, used to live, was living, were living
viv*íamos*	we lived, used to live, were living
viv*ían*	you, they lived, used to live, were living

There are only three verbs with irregular imperfects.

ir	to go	iba, iba, íbamos, iban
ser	to be	era, era, éramos, eran
ver	to see	veía, veía, veíamos, veían

Observe that in all verbs the first, second and third person singular imperfect are identical.

The following sentences will help to show the difference in use between the imperfect and the preterite.

Le *veía* todos los días.
I used to see him every day.

Le *vi* ayer.
I saw him yesterday.

¿Qué *hacía* usted cuando llamé?
What *were* you *doing* when I called?

¿Qué *hizo* usted cuando llamé?
What *did* you *do* when I called?

Cuando *éramos* chicos *íbamos* al cine todos los sábados.
When *we were* children, *we used to go* to the cinema every Saturday.

The preterite will be far more useful to you than the imperfect. The imperfect of the following verbs, however, is used more frequently than the preterite:

quería	I wanted	esperaba	I hoped
creía	I believed	tenía	I had
podía	I could	sabía	I knew

Creía que no *teníamos* el dinero.
He thought we hadn't got the money.

Quería verla.
I wanted to see her.

No *sabía* si *iban* a venir, pero lo *esperaba*.
I didn't know if *they were going* to come, but *I hoped* so.

The Present Perfect and Pluperfect

Just like English, Spanish has two compound past tenses, the present perfect (*I have spoken, I have seen*, etc.) and the pluperfect (*I had spoken, I had seen*, etc.). They are formed and used almost exactly as in English. The Spanish equivalent of the English auxiliary verb *have* is *haber*. Its present tense is

haber   to have (auxiliary)*   he, ha, hemos, han

The present perfect is formed by taking the present of *haber* and the past participle of a verb (formed by dropping the infinitive ending and adding *-ado* to the first conjugation and *-ido* to the second and third).

First conjugation   visitar (to visit)

he visitado	I have visited
ha visitado	you have visited, he, she, it has visited
hemos visitado	we have visited
han visitado	you, they have visited

Second conjugation

escoger (to choose)
he escogido	I have chosen

* In English the word *have* is also used to indicate possession. In Spanish *haber* is never used in this sense. *Tener* is used to indicate possession.

ha escogido	you have chosen, he, she, it has chosen
hemos escogido	we have chosen
han escogido	you, they have chosen

Third conjugation

insistir (to insist)

he insistido	I have insisted
ha insistido	you have insisted, he, she, it has insisted
hemos insistido	we have insisted
han insistido	you, they have insisted

The pluperfect tense is formed with the imperfect of *haber* (*había, había, habíamos, habían*) and the past participle.

gastar (to spend)

había gastado	I had spent
había gastado	you, he, she, it had spent
habíamos gastado	we had spent
habían gastado	they, you had spent

¿Han visitado Uds. el museo?
Have you visited the museum?

Hemos gastado mucho dinero.
We have spent a lot of money.

Nunca había vivido en un país extranjero.
I had never lived in a foreign country.

The following verbs have irregular past participles: abrir, abierto (opened); escribir, escrito (written); morir, muerto (died); poner, puesto (put); ver, visto (seen); volver, vuelto (returned); decir, dicho (said); hacer, hecho (done).

¿Qué *ha dicho* Ud.?
What *have* you *said*?

Ya *había muerto.*
He *had* already *died.*

¿Dónde *ha puesto* Ud. la llave?
Where *have* you *put* the key?

Remember that the preterite or simple past is the past
tense you should use most of the time. If you lack the time
to learn the other past tenses, you can get along without
them.

The Future Tense

The future tense is formed by adding *-é, -á, -emos, -án*
to the entire infinitive for all three conjugations.

First conjugation

	explicar (to explain)
explicar*é*	I shall explain
explicar*á*	you (SING.), he, she, it will explain
explicar*emos*	we shall explain
explicar*án*	you (PL.), they will explain

Second conjugation

	ver (to see)
ver*é*	I shall see
ver*á*	you, he, she, it will see
ver*emos*	we shall see
ver*án*	you, they will see

Third conjugation

	abrir (to open)
abrir*é*	I shall open
abrir*á*	you, he, she, it will open
abrir*emos*	we shall open
abrir*án*	they will open

The following common verbs have irregular stems in the future.

decir	to say, tell	diré, dirá, diremos, dirán
hacer	to do, make	haré, hará, haremos, harán
poder	to be able	podré, podrá, podremos, podrán
poner	to put, place	pondré, pondrá, pondremos, podrán
saber	to know	sabré, sabrá, sabremos, sabrán
salir	to leave	saldré, saldrá, saldremos, saldrán
tener	to have (possession)	tendré, tendrá, tendremos, tendrán
venir	to come	vendré, vendrá, vendremos, vendrán

Study the following sentences illustrating the use of the future which corresponds to English.

¿Qué *harán* ustedes mañana?
What *will* you *do* tomorrow?

No sé, pero creo que *podremos* visitar a algunos amigos.
I don't know but I think that *we'll be able* to visit some friends.

Volveremos temprano porque *iremos* al teatro después.
We'll return early because *we'll* go to the theatre later.

¿Cuándo *saldrá usted* para Guadalajara? Mañana si consigo boleto en el avión de la tarde; si no, *tendré* que tomar el autobús y no *llegaré* hasta el lunes.
When *will you leave* for Guadalajara? Tomorrow, if I get a ticket on the afternoon plane; if not, *I shall have* to take the bus and *shall* not *arrive* until Monday.

In English we frequently express the idea of futurity by using the verb *to go* with an infinitive. Similarly in Spanish we may use *ir a* with an infinitive.

¿Qué *van* ustedes *a* hacer?
What *are* you *going* to do?

Vamos a volver temprano porque *vamos a* ir al teatro después.
We're going to come back early because *we're going* to go to the theatre later.

Both in English and in Spanish we sometimes use the present tense instead of the future. For the beginner, this can be a useful alternative.

¿Qué *hacen Vds.* mañana?
What *are you doing* tomorrow?

¿Cuándo *sale Vd.* para Cuba?
When *are you leaving* for Cuba?

The Conditional

The conditional and past conditional are used as in English. To form the conditional add the endings *-ía*, *-ía*, *-íamos*, *-ían* to the infinitive for all three conjugations.

	ir (to go)
iría	I would go
iría	you, he, she, it would go
iríamos	we would go
irían	you, they would go

Verbs that have an irregular stem in the future have the same stem for the conditional:

diría	I would say, tell
haría	I would do, make

podría	I would be able
pondría	I would put
sabría	I would know
saldría	I would leave
tendría	I would have (possession)
vendría	I would come

To form the past conditional (*would have* and past participle in English) we take the conditional of *haber* and the past participle.

habría volado	I would have flown
habría volado	you, he, she, it would have flown
habríamos volado	we would have flown
habrían volado	you, they would have flown

Reflexive Verbs

In English we say *I got up at seven, I washed, shaved and dressed.* In Spanish, however, each of these verbs (*got up, washed, shaved, dressed*) must be used with a special reflexive pronoun; they are called reflexive verbs.

> Me levanté a las siete, me lavé, me afeité, y me vestí.
> (*Lit.*) I got myself up at seven, I washed myself, I shaved myself and I dressed myself.

Reflexive verbs are indicated in the dictionary by *-se* added to the infinitive: *levantarse, lavarse, vestirse.*

You need learn only three reflexive pronouns:

me	myself
se	yourself, himself, herself, itself, yourselves, themselves
nos	ourselves

These pronouns are placed in front of the verb in all forms except the infinitive and affirmative command, where they are placed directly on the end of the verb. We shall use the verb *sentarse, to sit down*, to illustrate the conjugation of a reflexive verb.

Present

me siento	I sit down
se sienta	you sit down, he, she, it sits down
nos sentamos	we sit down
se sientan	you, they sit down

Past

me senté	I sat down
se sentó	you, he, she, it sat down
nos sentamos	we sat down
se sentaron	you, they sat down

Future

me sentaré	I shall sit down
se sentará	you, he, she, it will sit down
nos sentaremos	we shall sit down
se sentarán	you, they will sit down

Commands

¡siénte*se* [Vd.]!	Sit down. (to one person)
¡siénten*se* [Vds.]!	Sit down. (to more than one person)
¡no *se* siente [Vd.]!	Don't sit down. (to one person)
¡no *se* sienten [Vds.]!	Don't sit down. (to more than one person)

Here is a list of the most important reflexive verbs. The *ie, ue* or *i* in parentheses indicates that the stem of the verb changes in the present.

acostarse (ue)	to go to bed
afeitarse	to shave
alegrarse	to be glad

casarse	to get married
despedirse (i)	to say good-bye
despertarse (ie)	to wake up
divertirse (ie)	to have a good time
lavarse	to wash (oneself)
levantarse	to get up
llamarse	to be called
ponerse	to put on
quejarse	to complain
quitarse	to take off
sentarse (ie)	to sit down
sentirse (ie)	to feel
vestirse (i)	to get dressed

Study the following examples which illustrate verbs used in non-reflexive and reflexive forms:

El barbero no me afeitó bien.
The barber didn't shave me well.

Me afeito todos los días.
I shave (myself) every day.

Llamé a mi amigo.
I called my friend.

¿Cómo *se* llama usted?
What is your name? (*Lit.* How do you call yourself?)

Me llamo Miguel Gómez.
My name is Michael Gómez. (*Lit.* I call myself Michael Gómez.)

Lavo los platos después de la comida.
I wash the dishes after dinner.

Me lavo las manos antes de comer.
I wash my hands before eating.

Other Examples of the Reflexive

In Spanish the reflexive is often used to express the English indefinite (*one*, *you*, *they* . . .) constructions and the passive (*to be* with a past participle). Note that the subject usually follows the verb in this construction.

Se habla portugués en el Brasil.
(*Lit.* Portuguese speaks itself in Brazil.)
They speak Portuguese in Brazil.
Portuguese is spoken in Brazil.
One speaks Portuguese in Brazil.

¿Cómo *se* dice esto en español?
(*Lit.* How does this say itself in Spanish?)
How do you say this in Spanish?
How is this said in Spanish?
How does one say this in Spanish?

¿Cómo *se* puede ir de aquí al centro?
(*Lit.* How is it possible to go from here to the main part of the town?)
How can one (I, you, we) go from here to the main part of the town?

Se prohibe fumar.
No smoking. Smoking is prohibited.

Se venden sombreros en esta tienda.
Hats are sold in this store.

El banco *se* cierra a las tres.
The bank closes (is closed) at three.

If, however, the person doing the action is expressed, we must use the true passive construction, which is the same as in English—the verb *to be* with a past participle. Note that the verb *to be* is translated by *ser* and that the past participle agrees with the subject in gender and number. Study the following examples:

> Las cartas *fueron escritas* por la secretaria.
> The letters *were written* by the secretary.
>
> Este edificio *fué construido* por mi compañía.
> This building *was constructed* by my company.

The Subjunctive

The subjunctive is very little used in English, but is quite frequent and important in Spanish. We are presenting briefly its formation and main uses, primarily for recognition when you see it or hear it, although correct use of the subjunctive in conversation is not difficult.

Formation of the Subjunctive Tenses; Present Subjunctive

We first came upon the subjunctive, without knowing it, when we learned the command form (p. 42), which is really part of the subjunctive. The present subjunctive of almost all verbs is formed by taking the first person singular (the *yo* form) of the present indicative (pp. 35–39), dropping the *-o*, and adding, for *-ar* verbs, *-e*, *-e*, *-emos*, *-en*; for *-er* and *-ir* verbs, *-a*, *-a*, *-amos*, *-an*:

INFINITIVE		1ST PERS. SING.	PRES. SUBJUNCTIVE
hablar	to speak	hablo	hable, hable, hablemos, hablen
comer	to eat	como	coma, coma, comamos, coman
escribir	to write	escribo	escriba, escriba, escribamos, escriban

Note the spelling changes necessary in verbs ending in *-car* and *-gar*:

INFINITIVE		1ST PERS. SING.	PRES. SUBJUNCTIVE
buscar	to seek	bus*co*	busque, busque, busquemos, busquen
pagar	to pay	pag*o*	pague, pague, paguemos, paguen

As with commands, verbs that are irregular in the first person singular of the present indicative (pp. 37–38) are irregular in the subjunctive. The following are the most important:

INFINITIVE		1ST PERS. SING.	PRES. SUBJUNCTIVE
decir	to say, tell	digo	diga, diga, digamos, digan
hacer	to do, make	hago	haga, haga, hagamos, hagan
oír	to hear	oigo	oiga, oiga, oigamos, oigan
poner	to put, place	pongo	ponga, ponga, pongamos, pongan
salir	to leave, go out	salgo	salga, salga, salgamos, salgan
tener	to have	tengo	tenga, tenga, tengamos, tengan
venir	to come	vengo	venga, venga, vengamos, vengan
ver	to see	veo	vea, vea, veamos, vean

Note the following irregular subjunctives not formed on the stem of the first person singular of the present indicative:

dar	to give	dé, dé, demos, den
estar	to be	esté, esté, estemos, estén
haber	to have (auxiliary)	haya, haya, hayamos, hayan
ir	to go	vaya, vaya, vayamos, vayan
saber	to know	sepa, sepa, sepamos, sepan
ser	to be	sea, sea, seamos, sean

The other tenses of the subjunctive are formed as follows:

Present Perfect Subjunctive

The present perfect subjunctive in Spanish is formed with the present subjunctive of the auxiliary verb *haber* and the past participle of the main verb:

hacer	to do, make	haya (haya, hayamos, hayan) hecho
ver	to see	haya (haya, hayamos, hayan) visto

Imperfect Subjunctive

The imperfect subjunctive is formed by dropping the *-ron* of the third person plural (the *ellos* form) of the preterite tense (pp. 43–45), and adding *-ra, -ra, -'ramos, -ran* or *-se, -se, -'semos, -sen*:*

INF.	3RD PERS. PL. PRETERITE		IMPERFECT SUBJUNCTIVE
hacer	hicieron		hiciera, hiciera, hiciéramos, hicieran
		OR	hiciese, hiciese, hiciésemos, hiciesen

Pluperfect Subjunctive

The pluperfect subjunctive is formed by placing the imperfect subjunctive of the auxiliary verb *haber* before the past participle of the main verb:

tomar	to take	hubiera, hubiera, hubiéramos, hubieran hubiese, hubiese, hubiésemos, hubiesen	}tomado

* These two forms may be used interchangeably, except that the *-se* form is not used in the if-clause of a conditional sentence. See paragraph 9 under "Uses of the Subjunctive".

Generally, if the verb in the main clause is in the present, future or command form the subjunctive verb will be in the present or present perfect; if the main verb is in the past the subjunctive will be imperfect or pluperfect. The model sentences in the following section will illustrate the uses of the tenses, as well as possible translations of the subjunctive.

Uses of the Subjunctive

The main uses of the subjunctive are as follows:

1. After the verb *querer* (to want) when there is a change of subject in the subordinate clause:

> Quiero que Vd. lo *haga*.
> I want you to *do* it. (*Lit.* I want that you *do* it.)
>
> Quería que Vd. lo *hiciera*.
> I wanted you to *do* it.

But use the infinitive as in English if there is no change of subject:

> Quiero *hacer*lo.
> I want *to do* it.

2. When one person *tells* (*decir*) or *asks* (*pedir*) another person to do something:

> Dígale que lo *escriba*.
> Tell him to *write* it.
>
> Me dijo que lo *escribiera*.
> He told me to *write* it.
>
> Nos piden que *salgamos*.
> They are asking us to *leave*.

3. After expressions of emotion, such as *esperar* (to hope), *sentir* (to be sorry), *temer* (to fear), *alegrarse* (to be glad), when there is a change of subject:

>Espero que *vuelvan*.
>I hope *they return*.
>
>Espero que *hayan vuelto*.
>I hope *they have returned*.
>
>Sentía que *vinieran*.
>I was sorry *they were coming*.
>
>Sentía que *hubieran venido*.
>I was sorry *they had come*.

BUT: Me alegro de *estar* aquí.
>I am glad *to be* here.

4. After *dudar* (to doubt) and other verbs expressing uncertainty:

>Dudo que lo *hagan*.
>I doubt that *they are doing it* (*they will do it*).
>
>Dudo que lo *hayan hecho*.
>I doubt that *they have done it*.
>
>Dudaba que lo *hicieran*.
>I doubted that *they were doing it* (*they would do it*).
>
>Dudaba que lo *hubieran hecho*.
>I doubted that *they had done it*.

5. After most impersonal expressions, such as *es posible* (it is possible), *es importante* (it is important), *es necesario*, *es preciso* (it is necessary), *es natural* (it is natural), if there is a subject for the subordinate verb:

>Es posible que *vayan*.
>It is possible that *they will go*.
>
>Era preciso que *fueran*.
>It was necessary for them to *go*.

Es natural que Vd. *diga* eso.
It is natural for you to *say* that.

BUT: Es imposible *hacerlo*.
It is impossible *to do* it.

6. In adjective clauses if the antecedent is indefinite:

Busco a alguien que *hable* inglés.
I am looking for someone who *speaks* English.

7. After certain adverbial conjunctions, such as *para que* (in order that), *sin que* (without), *antes que* (before):

Lo repite para que todos *entiendan*.
He is repeating it so that everyone *may understand*.

Salió sin que nadie le *viera*.
He left without anyone *seeing* him.

Lo haré antes que *vuelvan*.
I shall do it before *they return*.

8. After time conjunctions, such as *cuando* (when), *en cuanto* (as soon as), *hasta que* (until), when futurity is implied:

Cuando le *vea*, se lo diré.
When *I see* him, I shall tell it to him.

BUT: Cuando le *vi*, se lo dije.
When *I saw* him, I told it to him.

9. In contrary-to-fact conditions, the imperfect or pluperfect subjunctive must be used in the if-clause, with the conditional or past conditional, respectively, in the main clause (only the *-ra* forms are used in conditions):

Si *tuviera* el dinero, lo compraría.
If *I had* the money, I would buy it.

Si *hubiera tenido* el dinero, lo habría comprado.
If *I had had* the money, I would have bought it.

10. The *-ra* imperfect subjunctive forms of three verbs are often used with a conditional value in a main clause:

querer—quisiera	I would like
deber—debiera	I should, I ought to
poder—pudiera	I could, would be able to

Quisiéramos ir con Vd.
We *would like* to go with you.

Vds. *debieran* visitarlo.
You *ought* to visit it.

¿*Pudiera* Vd. ayudarme?
Could you help me?

Special Constructions with Verbs

English and Spanish have many parallel constructions, but each one also has many idiomatic constructions which cannot be translated literally from one language to the other. In the next few pages we shall call attention to the most useful of these special expressions.

The Verb *Gustar*

The English verb *to like* is usually translated by the Spanish verb *gustar*, *to please*. The sentence, *I like this city*, must be changed mentally to *This city pleases me*, before putting it into Spanish. The subject generally comes at the end of the sentence in this construction.

Me gusta esta ciudad.
I like this city. (*Lit.* This city pleases me.)

No me gusta.
I don't like it. (*Lit.* It does not please me.)

Le gustan mucho.
He likes them very much.

Nos gusta viajar.
We like to travel.

Me gustaría ir a Sevilla.
I would like to go to Seville.

When eating in someone's presence, you must offer some of your food by saying *¿Gusta?*, *Will you have some?*

Courtesy demands that the offer be declined by saying *Gracias, que le aproveche, Thank you, good appetite.*

The Verb *Hacer*

In addition to being one of the common verbs in the language, *hacer, to do, make* is also used in a variety of idiomatic constructions. Here are the most useful of these expressions.

1. Expressions of weather.

¿Qué tiempo hace?	How is the weather?
Hace buen (mal) tiempo.	The weather is fine (bad).
Hace frío.	It's cold.
Hace mucho calor.	It's very warm.
No hace mucho sol.	It's not very sunny.
But:	
Está lloviendo.	It's raining.
Está nevando.	It's snowing.

2. To translate the English *ago* we use the third person singular of *hacer* and the length of time.

Llegué hace tres días.	I arrived three days ago.

3. Action continued from the past to the present. To express an action that began in the past and still continues, we use the following formula: *Hace + time + que + verb in present tense.*

Hace mucho tiempo que viven aquí.
They have been living here for a long time. (*Lit.* It makes much time that they live here.)

Hace más de dos horas que espero.
I've been waiting more than two hours. (*Lit.* It makes more than two hours that I wait.)

The ordinary present perfect tense may be used as in English to express these ideas instead of the *hace* construction.

Han vivido aquí mucho tiempo.
They've lived here a long time.

He esperado más de dos horas.
I've waited more than two hours.

4. Note also the following idiomatic uses of *hacer*:

Hacer un viaje.	To take a trip.
Hacer una maleta.	To pack a suitcase.
Se hace tarde.	It's getting late.
No le hace.	It makes no difference.
No haga caso.	Don't pay attention to it.
Se hizo rico.	He became rich.
Se hizo daño al caer.	He hurt himself on falling.
Si me hace el favor.	Please.

Hay and *Había*

Hay translates *there is* and *there are*; *había* translates *there was* and *there were*.

Hay muchos turistas este año.
There are many tourists this year.

Había tantas cosas que ver.
There were so many things to see.

Hay que with the infinitive translates *it is necessary, one must.*

Hay que levantarse temprano mañana.
It is necessary to get up early tomorrow. *We must* get up early tomorrow.

Hay que dejar la cámara con el empleado.
One has to leave the camera with the employee.

Es necesario with the infinitive has the same meaning, however, and is easier to use.

Es necesario pasar por la aduana en la frontera.
It is necessary to go through the customs at the border.

The Verb *Tener*

To be hungry, thirsty, warm, etc., are rendered in Spanish by *to have hunger, thirst, warmth*, etc. The verb *tener, to have*, is used in these expressions.

Tengo (mucha) hambre.	I am (very) hungry.
Tengo (mucha) sed.	I am (very) thirsty.
Tengo (mucho) calor.	I am (very) warm.
Tengo (mucho) frío.	I am (very) cold.
Tengo prisa.	I am in a hurry.
Tengo miedo.	I am afraid.
Tiene razón.	He is right.
No tiene razón.	He is wrong.
Tengo sueño.	I am sleepy.

Note also the following idioms:

¿Cuántos años tiene usted?
How old are you?
Tengo veintiocho años.
I am twenty-eight.
Tiene el pelo rubio y los ojos azules.
He has blond hair and blue eyes.
¿Qué tiene usted?
What's the matter with you?
No tengo nada.
Nothing. (*Lit.* I don't have anything.)

Tener que with the infinitive means *to have to, must.*

Usted *tiene que* dejar la propina esta vez.
You *have to* leave the tip this time.

Tenemos que volver temprano.
We must return early.

The verb *deber* with the infinitive is very often used to mean *must, should, ought to.*

Usted *debe dejar* dos pesos por lo menos.
You *should leave* at least two pesos.

¿A qué hora *debemos partir*?
At what time *are we supposed to leave*?

Ustedes *deben estudiar* si quieren aprender.
You *ought to study* if you want to learn.

Acabar de with the Infinitive

Spanish has a special verb which conveys the idea of the English expression *have just* plus the past participle. This is the present of *acabar de* with the infinitive.

Acabamos de llegar.   We have just arrived.

The Verb *Querer*

The verb *querer* can mean *to want, to wish* and *to love.*

¿Qué quiere usted?
What do you want?

No quiero buscarlo ahora.
I don't want to look for it now.

Quiero a María y no *quiero* partir sin ella.
I *love* Mary and I don't *want* to leave without her.

A special form of this verb, *quisiera, I should like*, is more polite than *quiero, I want*, and is often used instead of it.

> *Quisiera* otra taza de café.
> *I should like* another cup of coffee.

> *Quisiera* presentarle a mi tío.
> *I'd like* to introduce you to my uncle.

Notice the following idioms:

> ¿Qué quiere Vd. decir?
> What do you mean?

> ¿Qué quiere decir esta palabra?
> What does this word mean?

> ¿Qué significa esta palabra?
> What does this word mean?

> Como Vd. quiera.
> As you wish.

The Verbs *Saber* and *Conocer*

In English we use the same word, *to know*, for both knowing facts and knowing people. In Spanish, however, these ideas are separated. *Conocer* means *to know* in the sense of being acquainted with persons and places, while *saber* means *to know* facts. *Conocer* may also mean to meet, to make the acquaintance of. Both verbs are irregular in the first person singular of the present. *Saber* has *sé*, and *conocer* has *conozco*.

> ¿Quién sabe?
> Who knows?

> Sólo Dios sabe.
> Only God knows.

¿Sabe Vd. la fecha?
Do you know the date?

No la conozco, pero quisiera conocerla.
I do not know her, but I'd like to meet her.

Mucho gusto en conocerle.
Pleased to meet you.

Le conocí el año pasado.
I met him last year.

Basic Verbs and Infinitives

In the last few pages dealing with special verbs it has been shown that by combining many verbs with an infinitive we can express a great variety of ideas. Let us mention again some of the most important of these verbs.

ir a	to be going to	
tener que	to have to	
querer	to want to, wish to	and infinitive
poder	to be able to	
deber	to have to, ought to	
acabar de	to have just	and past participle

Here are some more illustrative sentences:

¿Va usted a estudiar?
Are you going to study?

Voy a leer el periódico.
I am going to read the paper.

Tengo que dejarlo para mañana.
I have to leave it for tomorrow.

¿Quiere usted ayudarme?
Will you help me?

Quisiera ir al cine.
I would like to go to the movies.

No puedo salir hoy.
I cannot go out today.

¿Puede usted prestarme cien pesos?
Can you lend me a hundred pesos?

Debemos levantarnos temprano.
We have to get up early.

Acaban de entrar.
They have just come in.

Prepositions and Infinitives

In English we often use the present participle after a preposition (before *leaving*, after *eating*, without *thinking*, etc.). This is never done in Spanish. Only the infinitive form of the verb may follow a preposition.

antes de salir	before leaving
después de llegar	after arriving
para trabajar	in order to work
sin hablar	without speaking
al entrar	on entering

Some Useful Expressions

Here are some useful idiomatic expressions which have not appeared in the main body of this little grammar.

¿Qué hora es? Son las ocho y media.
What time is it? It is eight-thirty.

Echo de menos a mis padres. (echar de menos)
I miss my parents. (to miss)

Dar un paseo.	To take a walk. (or a drive)
No importa.	It doesn't matter.
No se preocupe.	Don't trouble yourself. (or don't worry)
Lo siento mucho.	I'm very sorry.
Está bien.	O.K., all right.
Es Vd. muy amable.	You're very kind.
Que se divierta.	Have a good time.
¡No me diga!	You don't say!
No sirve.	It's no good.
Buenos días.	Good morning.
Buenas tardes.	Good afternoon.
Buenas noches.	Good evening, good night.
¿Qué tal?	How are you? (to a friend)
Hasta luego.	See you later.
Hasta mañana.	See you tomorrow.
Por la mañana.	In the morning.
Por la tarde.	In the afternoon.
Por la noche.	In the evening.
Pasado mañana.	The day after tomorrow.

Mañana por la mañana.	Tomorrow morning.
A tiempo.	On time.
En seguida.	At once.
Al fin.	At last, finally.
Otra vez.	Again.
En vez de.	Instead of.
Pues.	Well.
Quizás.	Perhaps.
Por eso.	Therefore.
Por lo menos.	At least.
Por supuesto.	Of course.
¡Cómo no!	Of course.
Claro.	Of course.
Todo el mundo.	Everybody.
Con mucho gusto.	With pleasure.
Muchas gracias.	Many thanks.
De nada.	You're welcome.
Con permiso.	Excuse me. (with your permission)
Perdóneme.	Excuse me, pardon me.

Vocabulary Tips

Many words in English and Spanish are exactly the same for both languages. Many others have only minor changes in spelling, and are easily recognized. Study the following vocabulary hints and word lists.

1. Examples of words that are the same in both languages.

crisis	drama	error	general
metal	probable	tropical	variable

2. Some words add a final *-e*, *-a* or *-o* to the English word.

client*e*	artist*a*	absolut*o*
evident*e*	emblem*a*	contact*o*
ignorant*e*	pianist*a*	defect*o*
important*e*	problem*a*	líquid*o*
part*e*	sistem*a*	pretext*o*

3. The English ending *-ty* is usually the same as the Spanish *-tad* or *-dad*.

ciu*dad*	curiosi*dad*	liber*tad*	socie*dad*

4. English *-y* often corresponds to Spanish *-ía*, *-ia* or *-io*.

compañ*ía*	histor*ia*	diccionar*io*
geograf*ía*	farmac*ia*	ordinar*io*

5. English *-tion* equals Spanish *-ción*.

acción administración función

6. English *-ous* if often Spanish *-oso*.

delicioso famoso generoso precioso

Vocabulary Building with Cognates

When you study a foreign language, building a vocabulary is often one of the most difficult and laborious tasks. It can mean a great deal of tedious memorization and time-consuming study. Yet an English-speaker is in a fortunate position for learning foreign vocabulary, and his work can be considerably lightened. English is composite in origin, and in its immense vocabulary are to be found thousands of forms that are borrowed from other languages. If you have already studied a foreign language you probably remember the pleasure you felt when you came upon a word that was like its English counterpart; it immediately became easy to remember and use, since it was linked to something familiar, and it probably stayed in your memory longer than other words.

This word list is based upon a useful principle that is not widely used—the seeking out of vocabulary resemblances and making full use of them. It would seem to be obvious that the easiest way to obtain a Spanish vocabulary would be to study words that English shares with Spanish. Yet, surprisingly enough, until this present list, there has been no systematic compilation of the words that form the common ground between English and Spanish.

This list contains more than twenty-four hundred Spanish words, together with an equal number of English words that have the same meaning, and are either identical or very close in spelling to the Spanish. Most of these words are cognates, the Spanish words being derived from Latin, while the comparable English words have come either from literary Latin or indirectly through French or Italian. Some of the words in this list, however, are not cognates, but are simple borrowings. You are probably already familiar with such English borrowings from Spanish in such words as *sombrero*, *fiesta* and *siesta*. There are probably even more words, like *automóvil*, *eléctrico* and *tren* (train), which have moved from English into Spanish.

These twenty-four hundred words are the most frequently used words that English and Spanish have in common parallel forms. They are all important words in Spanish, all appearing among the top six thousand words in word-frequency counts. This list has been based upon a study of comparative cognates between English, French and Spanish, submitted by William E. Johnson, Jr., as a master's thesis to the George Peabody School for Teachers. The editors of Dover Publications have collated it with Helen S. Eaton's *Semantic Frequency List* and have enlarged it accordingly. While this list does not contain all the most common words in Spanish (since there are many Spanish words that do not have parallel English forms), it will give you many of the words that you are likely to need, and will enable you to express your needs in the easiest way.

Do not go beyond the words in this list, however, in assuming that English and Spanish words that look alike have the same meaning. There are many false analogies between the two languages, and it is not always safe to guess at Spanish words because of their appearance. Many words which were once related in the past have since drifted apart in meaning, and in many other words there were simply chance resemblances between English and Spanish. The Spanish word *largo* does not mean large; it means long.

If you concentrate on the twenty-four hundred words of this list you will find that you will be able to comprehend a good deal of Spanish, and will be able to express your thoughts with a minimum of memorization. Learn to recast your thoughts in these words when you speak. Instead of thinking (in English) of big and great and large, think of grand, which is close to Spanish *grande*; instead of thinking of minute, think of moment; instead of let, think of permit. Each of these words has its cognate or near equivalent in Spanish, and you will be able to express yourself without ambiguities or mis-statements.

Use whatever methods come easiest to you for learning these words. Some language experts advise you simply to read through the list two or three times a day for several weeks, and then to let your mind pick up words unconsciously. The association between English and Spanish in this list is so close, that simply reading and re-reading the list will enlarge your vocabulary by hundreds of useful words. Some teachers recommend that you memorize a certain number of words each day, perhaps making sentences with them. There aren't many short cuts to learning and study. This is one of the few of real value. Do not be afraid of making mistakes. You may be unidiomatic at times; you may be grammatically incorrect occasionally; but you will probably be understood.

Table of Common Equivalents

Spanish	English	Examples	
-mente	-ly	absoluta*mente*	absolute*ly*
-dad	-ty	necesi*dad*	necessi*ty*
-ción	-tion	condi*ción*	condi*tion*
-ie- (sometimes)	-e-	m*ie*mbra	m*e*mber
-ue- (sometimes)	-o-	c*ue*rpo	c*o*rpse
v	b	automó*v*il	automo*b*ile
f	ph	*f*rase	*ph*rase

List of Cognates

abandon	abandonar	accuse	acusar
abdicate	abdicar	accustom	acostumbrar
abnormal	abnormal	acid	ácido
abolish	abolir	acquire	adquirir
abolition	abolición	acquisition	adquisición
abominable	abominable	act (n.)	acto
abound	abundar	act (v.)	actuar
abrupt	abrupto	actuate	actuar
absolute	absoluto	action	acción
absolutely	absolutamente	active	activo
absorb	absorber	activity	actividad
abstain	abstener (se)	actor	actor
abstraction	abstracción	actress	actriz
absurd	absurdo	actuality	actualidad
abundance	abundancia	adapt	adaptar
abundant	abundante	addition	adición
abundantly	abundantemente	adhere	adherir
abuse (n.)	abuso	adherent	adherente
abuse (v.)	abusar	adjust	ajustar
abyss	abismo	administrate	administrar
academy	academia	administration	administración
accelerate	accelerar	administrative	administrativo
accent	acento	administrator	administrador
accentuate	acentuar	admirable	admirable
acceptance	aceptación	admirably	admirablemente
access	acceso	admiration	admiración
accessory	accesorio	admire	admirar
accident	accidente	admit	admitir
acclaim (v.)	aclamar	admonish	amonestar
accompany	acompañar	adolescence	adolescencia
accord (n.)	acuerdo	adolescent	adolescente
accumulate	acumular	adopt	adoptar
accusation	acusación	adoption	adopción

adoration	adoración	align	alinear
adore	adorar	aliment	alimento
adulation	adulación	alimentation	alimentación
adult (*adj.*) (*n.*)	adulto	allege	alegar
advance (*n.*)	avance	alleviate	aliviar
advance (*v.*)	avanzar	alliance	alianza
adventure	aventura	allusion	alusión
adventurer	aventurero	altar	altar
adverb	adverbio	alter	alterar
adversary	adversario	alteration	alteración
adverse	adverso	alternate (*v.*)	alternar
adversity	adversidad	alternately	alternativamente
aesthetic	estético	amass	amasar
affable	afable	amber	ámbar
affect (*v.*)	afectar	ambition	ambición
affection	afección	ambitious	ambicioso
affirm	afirmar	ameliorate	ameliorar
affirmation	afirmación	American	americano
affirmative	afirmativo	amiability	amabilidad
affliction	aflicción	amicable	amigable
agency	agencia	amplify	amplificar
agent	agente	analogous	análogo
aggravate	agravar	analogy	analogía
aggregate (*v.*)	agregar	analysis	análisis
aggression	agresión	analyse	analizar
aggressive	agresivo	anarchy	anarquía
aggressor	agresor	anecdote	anécdota
agile	ágil	angel	ángel
agitate	agitar	angle	ángulo
agitation	agitación	anguish	angustia
agony	agonía	animal	animal
agreeable	agradable	animate	animar
agricultural	agrícola	animation	animación
agriculture	agricultura	annex (*n.*)	anexo
ah!	¡ah!	anniversary	aniversario
air (*n.*)	aire	announce	anunciar
alarm (*v.*)	alarmar	annual	anual
album	álbum	annul	anular
alcohol	alcohol	anonymous	anónimo
alcoholic	alcohólico	antecedent	antecedente
alert	alerta	anterior	anterior

anticipate	anticipar	arrogance	arrogancia
antique	antiquo	arrogant	arrogante
antiquity	antigüedad	art	arte
aplomb	aplomo	article	artículo
apostle	apóstol	articulate	articular
apostolic	apostólico	articulation	articulación
apparatus	aparato	artificial	artificial
apparent	aparente	artillery	artillería
apparition	aparición	artist	artista
appeal (v.)	apelar	artistic	artístico
appear	aparecer	ascend	ascender
appendix	apéndice	ascension	ascensión
appetite	apetito	aspect	aspecto
applaud	aplaudir	aspiration	aspiración
applause	aplauso	aspire	aspirar
applicable	aplicable	assassin	asesino
application	aplicación	assassinate	asesinar
apply	aplicar	assembly	asamblea
apprehension	aprehensión	assimilate	asimilar
apprentice	aprendiz	assistance	asistencia
approbation	aprobación	associate (v.)	asociar
appropriate (v.)	apropiar	association	asociación
approve	aprobar	assume	asumir
approximate	aproximar	astronomer	astrónomo
aptitude	aptitud	athlete	atleta
arbitrariness	arbitrariedad	athletic	atlético
arbitrary	arbitrario	atmosphere	atmósfera
arbitrator	arbitrador	atom	átomo
arcade	arcada	atrocity	atrocidad
arch	arco	attack (n.)	ataque
archipelago	archipiélago	attack (v.)	atacar
architect	arquitecto	attention	attención
architecture	arquitectura	attentive	atento
ardour	ardor	attentively	atentivamente
arduous	ardoroso	attenuate	atenuar
argument	argumento	attic	ático
arid	árido	attitude	actitud
aristocracy	aristocracia	attraction	atracción
aristocratic	aristocrático	attractive	atractivo
arm (v.)	armar	attribute (n.)	atributo
aroma	aroma	attribute (v.)	atribuir

audacious	audaz
audacity	audacia
audience	audiencia
augment	aumentar
augmentation	aumentación
august	augusto
aurora	aurora
austere	austero
austerity	austeridad
authentic	auténtico
author	autor
authority	autoridad
authorization	autorización
authorize	autorizar
automatic	automático
automaton	autómata
automobile	automóvil
autonomy	autonomía
auxiliary	auxiliar
avarice	avaricia
avenue	avenida
aversion	aversión
avid	ávido
azure	azul
bah!	¡bah!
balance (n.)	balanza
balance (v.)	balancear
balcony	balcón
balloon	balón
band	banda
bandit	bandido
bank	banco
banker	banquero
banquet	banquete
bar	barra
barbarian	bárbaro
barbarity	barbaridad
barber	barbero
bark	barca
baron	barón

barrel	barril
base	base
bastard	bastardo
battalion	batallón
battery	batería
battle	batalla
bayonet	bayoneta
benediction	bendición
benefice	beneficio
beneficent	benéfico
benefit (n.)	beneficio
benefit (v.)	beneficiar
benevolence	benevolencia
benevolent	benévolo
benign	benigno
biblical	bíblico
bicycle	bicicleta
biography	biografía
bland	blando
blasphemy	blasfemia
blouse	blusa
boat	bote
bomb	bomba
border	borde
boulevard	bulevar
bourgeois	burgués
boxer	boxeador
brave	bravo
bravely	bravamente
bravery	bravura
bravo	bravo
brigade	brigada
brilliant	brillante
Britannic	británico
bronze	bronce
brutal	brutal
brutality	brutalidad
brutally	brutalmente
brute	bruto
burlesque	burlesco
bust	busto

cable	cable	catholicism	catolicismo
cadaver	cadáver	cause (*n.*)	causa
café	café	cause (*v.*)	causar
calculate	calcular	cease	cesar
calculation	cálculo	cede	ceder
calendar	calendario	celebrate	celebrar
calm (*v.*)	calmar	celestial	celeste
calumny	calumnia	cement	cemento
Calvary	calvario	centre	centro
camel	camello	central	central
canal	canal	ceremony	ceremonia
canape	canapé	certificate	certificado
canary	canario	champagne	champaña
candid	cándido	champion	campeón
candidacy	candidatura	chaos	caos
candidate	candidato	character	carácter
candour	candor	characteristic	característico
canon	canón	characterize	caracterizar
canton	cantón	charity	caridad
capacity	capacidad	chastity	castidad
cape	capa	chauffeur	chauffeur
capital	capital	cheque (*n.*)	cheque
caprice	capricho	chic	chic
capricious	caprichoso	chimney	chimenea
captain	capitán	chocolate	chocolate
capture	capturar	Christian	cristiano
caravan	caravana	chronicle	crónica
cardinal	cardinal	cigar	cigarro
career	carrera	cigarette	cigarrillo
carpenter	carpintero	circle	círculo
carton	cartón	circuit	circuito
cascade	cascada	circular (*adj.*)	circular
case	caso	circulate	circular
caste	casta	circulation	circulación
castigate	castigar	circumstance	circumstancia
casual	casual	circus	circo
catalogue	catálogo	citation	citación
catastrophe	catástrofe	cite	citar
category	categoría	civilization	civilización
cathedral	catedral	civilize	civilizar
catholic	católico	class	clase

classic	clásico
classify	clasificar
clemency	clemencia
clement	clemente
client	cliente
clientèle	clientela
climate	clima
club	club
code	código
cohesion	cohesión
coincide	coincidir
coincidence	coincidencia
collaborate	colaborar
collaboration	colaboración
collaborator	colaborador
colleague	colega
collection	colección
collectivity	colectividad
colonial	colonial
colony	colonia
colour (n.)	color
colour (v.)	colorar
coloured	colorado
colossal	colosal
colossus	coloso
column	columna
combat (n.)	combate
combat (v.)	combatir
combination	combinación
combine	combinar
combustion	combustión
comedian	comediante
comedy	comedia
comical	cómico
commandant	comandante
commence	comenzar
commentary	comentario
commerce	comercio
commercial	comercial
commissary	comisario
commission	comisión

commit	cometer
common	común
communicate	comunicar
communication	comunicación
communion	comunión
community	comunidad
company	compañía
comparable	comparable
compare	comparar
comparison	comparación
compassion	compasión
compatriot	compatriota
compensation	compensación
complement	complemento
complete (adj.)	completo
complete (v.)	completar
completely	completamente
complex	complejo
complicate	complicar
complicated	complicado
complication	complicación
complicity	complicidad
compliment	complimento
comport (v.)	comportar
composition	composición
comprehend	comprender
compromise (n.)	compromiso
comrade	camarada
concede	conceder
conceive	concebir
concentrate	concentrar
concentration	concentración
concept	concepto
conception	concepción
concert	concierto
concession	concesión
conciliate	conciliar
conciliation	conciliación
conclude	concluir
conclusion	conclusión
concourse	concurso

concrete	concreto	consonant	consonante
concurrence	concurrencia	conspirator	conspirador
condemnation	condenación	conspire	conspirar
condense	condensar	constant	constante
condition	condición	constitute	constituir
conduct (*n.*)	conducta	constitution	constitución
conductor	conductor	constitutional	constitucional
confederation	confederación	construct	construir
confer	conferir	construction	construción
conference	conferencia	consul (*n.*)	cónsul
confess	confesar	consult	consultar
confession	confesión	consume	consumir
confessor	confesor	consummation	consumación
confidence	confianza	contact	contacto
confident (*n.*)	confidente	contagious	contagioso
confidential	confidencial	contain	contener
confine (*v.*)	confinar	contaminate	contaminar
confirm	confirmar	contemplate	contemplar
confirmation	confirmación	contemplation	contemplación
conflict	conflicto	contemporary	contemporáneo
conform	conforme	contend	contender
confusion	confusión	content	contento
congress	congreso	continent	continente
conjure	conjurar	continual	continuo
conquer	conquistar	continually	continuamente
conquest	conquista	continuation	continuación
conscience	conciencia	continue	continuar
consecration	consagración	contract	contrato
consent (*n.*)	consentimiento	contraction	contracción
consent (*v.*)	consentir	contradict	contradecir
consequence	consecuencia	contradiction	contradicción
conservation	conservación	contrarily	contrariamente
conserve	conservar	contrary	contrario
consider	considerar	contrast (*n.*)	contraste
considerable	considerable	contrast (*v.*)	contrastar
consideration	consideración	contribute	contribuir
consign	consignar	contribution	contribución
consist	consistir	control (*n.*)	control
consolation	consolación	convention	convención
console	consolar	conversation	conversación
consolidate	consolidar	converse (*v.*)	conversar

conversion	conversión	cruelly	cruelmente
convert (n.)	converto	crystal	cristal
convert (v.)	convertir	Cuban	cubano
conviction	convicción	cube	cubo
convince	convencer	cultivate	cultivar
convoke	convocar	cultivator	cultivador
co-operative	cooperativa	culture	cultura
copious	copioso	cupola	cúpula
copy (n.)	copia	curiosity	curiosidad
copy (v.)	copiar	curious	curioso
coral	coral	curve	curva
cordial	cordial	cylinder	cilindro
corporation	corporación	cypress	ciprés
correct (adj.)	correcto		
correction	corrección		
correctly	correctamente	dame	dama
correspond	corresponder	dance (n.)	danza
correspondence	correspondencia	dance (v.)	danzar
correspondent	correspondiente	date (v.)	datar
corridor	corredor	debate	debate
corruption	corrupción	debilitate	debilitar
cost (v.)	costar	debut	debut
count (v.)	contar	decade	década
course	curso	decadence	decadencia
courtesy	cortesía	decent	decente
cranium	cráneo	deception	decepción
cream	crema	decide	decidir
create	crear	decidedly	decididamente
creation	creación	decision	decisión
creator	creador	decisive	decisivo
creature	criatura	declaration	declaración
credit	crédito	declare	declarar
crepuscule	crepúsculo	decline	declinar
crest	cresta	decorate	decorar
crime	crimen	decoration	decoración
criminal	criminal	decree	decreto
crisis	crisis	dedicate	dedicar
critic	crítico	deduction	deducción
criticism	crítica	defect	defecto
crude	crudo	defective	defectuoso
cruel	cruel	defend	defender

defence	defensa	destination	destinación
define	definir	destine	destinar
definite	definitivo	destiny	destino
definition	definición	destroy	destrozar
degenerate	degenerar	destruction	destrucción
delegation	delegación	detail	detalle
deliberate	deliberar	determine	determinar
delicacy	delicadeza	detestable	detestable
delicate	delicado	detriment	detrimento
delicious	delicioso	devastate	devastar
delinquent	delincuente	devotion	devoción
delirium	delirio	devour	devorar
democracy	democracia	devout	devoto
democratic	democrático	dialogue	diálogo
demolish	demoler	diameter	diámetro
demon	demonio	diamond	diamante
demonstrate	demonstrar	dictate	dictar
demonstration	demonstración	dictionary	diccionario
denote	denotar	difference	diferencia
denounce	denunciar	different	diferente
dense	denso	difficult	difícil
density	densidad	difficulty (n.)	dificultad
denude	desnudar	difficulty (adv.)	difícilmente
department	departamento	diffusion	difusión
dependence	dependencia	digestion	digestión
deplorable	deplorable	dignity	dignidad
deplore	deplorar	diligence	diligencia
deposit	depositar	dimension	dimensión
despotism	despotismo	diocese	diócesis
derive	derivar	diplomatic	diplomático
descend	descender	direct	directo
describe	describir	direction	dirección
description	descripción	directly	directamente
desert (n.)	desierto	director	director
desert (v.)	desertar	disagreeable	desagradable
designate	designar	disarm	desarmar
desire (v.)	desear	disaster	desastre
desist	desistir	disc	disco
despair	desesperar	discern	discernir
desperation	desesperación	disciple	discípulo
despot	déspota	discipline	disciplina

disconcert	desconcertar	divulge	divulgar
disconsolate	desconsolado	docile	dócil
discontent	descontento	doctor	doctor
discord	discordia	doctrine	doctrina
discourse	discurso	document	documento
discreet	discreto	dogma	dogma
discreetly	discretamente	domicile	domicilio
discretion	discreción	dominate	dominar
discuss	discutir	domination	dominación
discussion	discusión	dormitory	dormitorio
disembark	desembarcar	double (*adj.*)	doble
disgrace	desgracia	double (*v.*)	doblar
disgust (*v.*)	disgustar	dragon	dragón
dishonour (*n.*)	deshonor	drama	drama
disorder (*n.*)	desorden	dramatic	dramático
dispatch	despacho	duel	duelo
dispense	dispensar	duke	duque
disperse	dispersar	durable	durable
disposition	disposición	duration	duración
dispute (*n*).	disputa	dynasty	dinastía
dispute (*v.*)	disputar		
dissolution	disolución	eccentric	excéntrico
dissolve	disolver	eccentricity	excentricidad
distance	distancia	ecclesiastical	eclesiástico
distant	distante	echo	eco
distillation	destilación	economic	económico
distillery	destilería	economy	economía
distinct	distinto	edict	edicto
distinction	distinción	edifice	edificio
distinguish	distinguir	edify	edificar
distraction	distracción	edition	edición
distribute	distribuir	education	educación
distribution	distribución	effect	efecto
divan	diván	effective	efectivo
divergence	divergencia	efficacy	eficacia
diversion	diversión	effusion	efusión
divert	divertir	egoism	egoísmo
divine (*n.*)	divino	egoist	egoísta
divine (*v.*)	adivinar	elaboration	elaboración
division	división	elastic	elástico
divorce (*v.*)	divorciar	election	elección

elector	elector	equality	igualdad
electoral	electoral	equilibrate	equilibrar
electric	eléctrico	equilibrium	equilibrio
electricity	electricidad	equity	equidad
elegance	elegancia	equivalent	equivalente
elegant	elegante	era	era
element	elemento	err	errar
elevate	elevar	errant	errante
elevation	elevación	error	error
eliminate	eliminar	erudition	erudición
eloquence	elocuencia	essence	esencia
eloquent	elocuente	essential	esencial
emanate	emanar	essentially	esencialmente
emancipate	emancipar	establish	establecer
embalm	embalsamar	establishment	establecimiento
embark	embarcar	estimable	estimable
emblem	emblema	eternal	eterno
emigrant	emigrante	eternally	eternamente
emigration	emigración	eternity	eternidad
eminent	eminente	evacuate	evacuar
emotion	emoción	evade	evadir
emperor	emperador	evaluate	evaluar
emphasis	énfasis	eventual	eventual
empire	imperio	evidence	evidencia
enemy	enemigo	evident	evidente
energetic	enérgico	evidently	evidentemente
energetically	enérgicamente	evoke	evocar
energy	energía	evolution	evolución
enervate	enervar	exact	exacto
engender	engendrar	exactitude	exactitud
enigma	enigma	exactly	exactamente
enormous	enorme	exaggerate	exagerar
enter	entrar	exaggeration	exageración
enthusiasm	entusiasmo	exalt	exaltar
enthusiast	entusiasta	exaltation	exaltación
entitle	intitular	examination	examen
enumerate	enumerar	examine	examinar
envy	envidia	excellence	excelencia
epicure	epicúreo	excellent	excelente
episode	episodio	except	excepto
epoch	época	exception	excepción

exceptional	excepcional	express (v.)	expresar
exceptionally	excepcional-	expression	expresión
	mente	expressive	expresivo
excess	exceso	expulsion	expulsión
excessive	excesivo	exquisite	exquisito
excessively	excesivamente	extension	extensión
excite	excitar	exterior	exterior
exclamation	exclamación	extinguish	extinguir
exclude	excluir	extra	extra
exclusive	exclusivo	extract	extracto
exclusively	exclusivamente	extraction	extracción
excursion	excursión	extraordinary	extraordinario
excuse (n.)	excusa	extreme	extremo
excuse (v.)	excusar	extremity	extremidad
executor	ejecutor		
exemption	exempción	fable	fábula
exhibit (v.)	exhibir	fabricate	fabricar
exhibition	exhibición	fabrication	fabricación
exigency	exigencia	fabulous	fabuloso
exist (v.)	existir	facilitate	facilitar
existence	existencia	facility	facilidad
exotic	exótico	faction	facción
expansion	expansión	factor	factor
expansive	expansivo	faculty	facultad
expedition	expedición	false	falso
expel	expulsar	falsify	falsear
experience	experiencia	falsity	falsedad
experiment (v.)	experimentar	fame	fama
experimental	experimental	familiarity	familiaridad
expert	experto	family	familia
expiation	expiación	famous	famoso
expire	expirar	fanaticism	fanatismo
explication	explicación	fantastic	fantástico
exploit (v.)	explotar	fantasy	fantasía
exploitation	explotación	fascinate	fascinar
exploration	exploración	fatality	fatalidad
explore	explorar	fatigue	fatiga
explosion	explosión	fatuous	fatuo
exportation	exportación	favour (n.)	favor
exposition	exposición	favour (v.)	favorecer
express (n.)	expreso	favourable	favorable

favourite (n., adj.)	favorito	fortify	fortificar
fecund	fecundo	fortunate	afortunado
federation	federación	fortune	fortuna
felicitate	felicitar	foundation	fundación
felicitation	felicitación	fraction	fracción
felicity	felicidad	fragile	frágil
feminine	feminino	fragment	fragmento
ferment (v.)	fermentar	fragrance	fragancia
ferocious	feroz	frank	franco
ferocity	ferocidad	frankly	francamente
fertile	fértil	frenetic	frenético
fervent	ferviente	frequent (adj.)	frecuente
fervour	fervor	frequent (v.)	frecuentar
festive	festivo	frequently	frecuentemente
fibre	fibra	fresh	fresco
fiction	ficción	frivolity	frivolidad
fidelity	fidelidad	frivolous	frívolo
figure (n.)	figura	frontier	frontera
filial	filial	fruit	fruta
final	final	fruiterer	frutero
finally	finalmente	frustrate	frustrar
finance	finanza	fugitive	fugitivo
financial	financiero	function (n.)	función
fine	fino	function (v.)	funcionar
firm (adj.)	firme	functionary	funcionario
firmament	firmamento	fundament	fundamento
flagrant	flagrante	fundamental	fundamental
flexibility	flexibilidad	funeral	funeral
float	flotar	furious	furioso
fluid	flúido	furtive	furtivo
foment	fomentar	fury	furia / furor
force (v.)	forzar		
forced	forzado	gallant	galante
form (n.)	forma	gallery	galería
form (v.)	formar	gallop	galope
formality	formalidad	gardener	jardinero
formation	formación	gas	gas
formidable	formidable	gasoline	gasolina
formula	formula	gendarme	gendarme
formulate	formular	general (n.)	general

general (*adj.*)	general	group (*n.*)	grupo
generality	generalidad	group (*v.*)	agrupar
generalize	generalizar	guarantee (*n.*)	garantía
generally	generalmente	guarantee (*v.*)	garantizar
generation	generación	guard (*n.*)	guardia
generosity	generosidad	guillotine	guillotina
generous	generoso	guitar	guitarra
genius	génio	gusto	gusto
genteel	gentil	gymnasium	gimnasio
gentility	gentileza	gyrate	girar
genuine	genuino		
geography	geografía	habit	hábito
geometrical	geométrico	habitation	habitación
geranium	geranio	habitual	habitual
germ	germen	habitually	habitualmente
germinate	germinar	hatchet	hacha
gesticulate	gesticular	harmonious	armonioso
gesture	gesto	harmony	armonía
giant	gigante	heir	heredero
gigantic	gigantesco	hemisphere	hemisferio
glacial	glacial	herb	hierba
globe	globo	heresy	herejía
glorious	glorioso	heretic	herético
glory	gloria	hereditary	hereditario
golf	golf	hero	héroe
gothic	gótico	heroic	heróico
gourmet	gourmet	heroism	heroísmo
gracious	gracioso	historian	historiador
gradual	gradual	historic	histórico
graduate (*v.*)	graduar	history	historia
grain	grano	homicide	homicidio
grammar	gramática	homogeneous	homogéneo
grandeur	grandeza	honest	honesto
granite	granito	honesty	honestidad
graphic	gráfico	honour	honor
gratify	gratificar	honourable	honorable
gratis	gratis	horizon	horizonte
gratitude	gratitud	horizontal	horizontal
grave (*adj.*)	grave	horrendous	horrendo
gravely	gravemente	horrible	horrible
grotesque	grotesco	horribly	horriblemente

horror	horror	imitation	imitación
hospital	hospital	immediate	inmediato
hospitality	hospitalidad	immediately	immediatamente
hostile	hostil	immense	inmenso
hostility	hostilidad	immensity	inmensidad
hotel	hotel	imminent	inminente
human	humano	immobility	inmovilidad
humanity	humanidad	immolate	inmolar
humid	húmedo	immortal	inmortal
humiliate	humillar	impartial	imparcial
humiliation	humillación	impassible	impasible
humility	humildad	impatience	impaciencia
humour	humor	imperative	imperativo
hurricane	huracán	imperceptible	imperceptible
hydrogen	hidrógeno	imperfect	imperfecto
hygiene	higiene	imperial	imperial
hypocrisy	hipocresía	impertinence	impertinencia
hypocrite	hipócrita	impetuous	impetuoso
hysterical	histérico	implacable	implacable
		implicate	implicar
		implore	implorar
idea	idea	import (v.)	importar
ideal	ideal	importance	importancia
identical	idéntico	important	importante
identity	identidad	importation	importación
idiot	idiota	importunate	importuno
ignoble	innoble	imposition	imposición
ignorance	ignorancia	impossibility	imposibilidad
ignorant	ignorante	impossible	imposible
illuminate	iluminar	impotence	impotencia
illusion	ilusión	impotent	impotente
illustrate	ilustrar	impregnate	impregnar
illustration	ilustración	impression	impresión
illustrous	ilustre	improvise	improvisar
image	imagen	imprudence	imprudencia
imaginary	imaginario	imprudent	imprudente
imagination	imaginación	impudent	impudente
imaginative	imaginativo	impulsion	impulsión
imagine	imaginar	impure	impuro
imbecile	imbécil	inaugurate	inaugurar
imitate	imitar	incapacity	incapacidad

incessant	incesante	inexplicable	inexplicable
incident	incidente	inextricable	inextricable
inclination	inclinación	infallible	infalible
incline (v.)	inclinar (se)	infamous	infame
incomparable	incomparable	infamy	infamia
incompatible	incompatible	infancy	infancia
incomplete	incompleto	infantile	infantil
incomprehensi-		infantry	infantería
ble	incomprensible	inferior	inferior
incontestable	incontestable	infernal	infernal
inconvenient	inconveniente	inferno	infierno
incorporate	incorporar	infinitely	infinitamente
incredible	increíble	infinity	infinidad
incurable	incurable	influence (n.)	influencia
indecision	indecisión	influence (v.)	influir
indefatigable	infatigable	influential	influente
indefinite	indefinido	inform (v.)	informar
independence	independencia	information	información
independent	independiente	ingenious	ingenioso
Indian	indiano	ingratitude	ingratitud
indicate	indicar	inhuman	inhumano
indication	indicación	initial	inicial
indicative	indicativo	initiative	iniciativo
indifference	indiferencia	injury	injuria
indifferent	indiferente	injustice	injusticia
indigenous	indígena	innocence	inocencia
indignation	indignación	innocent	inocente
indirect	indirecto	inoffensive	inofensivo
indiscreet	indiscreto	insane	insano
indiscretion	indiscreción	inscription	inscripción
indispensable	indispensable	insect	insecto
individual (n.)	individuo	insensible	insensible
individual (adj.)	individual	inseparable	inseparable
indolence	indolencia	insert	insertar
indulgence	indulgencia	insignificant	insignificante
indulgent	indulgente	insinuate	insinuar
industrial	industrial	insist	insistir
industry	industria	insistence	insistencia
inert	inerte	insolence	insolencia
inestimable	inestimable	insolent	insolente
inevitable	inevitable	inspection	inspección

inspector	inspector	interpreter	intérprete
inspiration	inspiración	interrogate	interrogar
inspire	inspirar	interrupt	interrumpir
install	instalar	interruption	interrupción
installation	instalación	interval	intervalo
instance	instancia	intervene	intervenir
instantaneously	instantánea-	intervention	intervención
	mente	interview	interviú
instinct	instinto	intimacy	intimidad
instinctive	instintivo	intimate	íntimo
instinctively	instintivamente	intimidate	intimidar
institute (n.)	instituto	intolerable	intolerable
institute (v.)	instituir	intonation	intonación
institution	institución	intrepid	intrépido
instruction	instrucción	intrigue	intriga
instrument	instrumento	introduce	introducir
insufficiency	insuficiencia	introduction	introducción
insufficient	insuficiente	intuition	intuición
insular	insular	inundate	inundar
insult (n.)	insulto	invade	invadir
insult (v.)	insultar	invariable	invariable
insuperable	insuperable	invasion	invasión
insupportable	insoportable	invent	inventar
insurgent	insurgente	invention	invención
intact	intacto	inverse	inverso
integral	integral	investigate	investigar
integrity	integridad	investigation	investigación
intellectual	intelectual	invisible	invisible
intelligence	inteligencia	invitation	invitación
intelligent	inteligente	invite	invitar
intense	intenso	invoke	invocar
intensity	intensidad	involuntary	involuntario
intent	intento	iris	iris
intention	intención	ironical	irónico
interest (n.)	interés	irony	ironía
interest (v.)	interesar (se)	irregular	irregular
interior	interior	irreparable	irreparable
interminable	interminable	irresistible	irresistible
international	internacional	irresolute	irresoluto
interpret	interpretar	irritate	irritar
interpretation	interpretación	irritation	irritación

irruption	irrupción	liberation	liberación
isle	isla	liberty	libertad
		limit	limitar
jar	jarra	limitation	limitación
jargon	jerga	limpid	límpido
jubilance	júbilo	line	línea
judicial	judicial	liquid	líquida
judiciary	judiciario	liquidate	liquidar
jurisdiction	jurisdicción	liquor	licor
jurisprudence	jurisprudencia	list	lista
just	justo	literary	literario
justice	justicia	literature	literatura
justify	justificar	livid	lívido
juvenile (*adj.*)	juvenil	locality	localidad
		locomotive	locomotora
kilogram	kilogramo	logical	lógico
kilometre	kilómetro	longitude	longitud
		lucid	lúcido
labour (*n.*)	labor	lugubrious	lúgubre
labour (*v.*)	laborar	luminous	luminoso
laboratory	laboratorio	lyric	lírico
laborious	laborioso		
labyrinth	laberinto	magic	mágico
lament	lamentar	magistrate	magistrado
lamentable	lamentable	magnetic	magnético
lamp	lámpara	magnificent	magnífico
lance	lanza	magnitude	magnitud
language	{ lengua / lenguaje }	majestic	majestuoso
		majesty	majestad
languid	lánguido	malediction	maldición
lassitude	lasitud	malice	malicia
latitude	latitud	malignant	maligno
laudable	laudable	mamma	mamá
laurel	laurel	mandate	mandato
legal	legal	mania	manía
legion	legión	manifest (*n.*)	manifiesto
legislation	legislación	manifest (*v.*)	manifestar
legislator	legislador	manifestation	manifestación
legitimate	legítimo	manner	manera
liberal	liberal	mansion	mansión
liberate	liberar	manual	manual

manuscript	manuscrito	merit	mérito
map	mapa	metal	metal
march (v.)	marchar	metallic	metálico
margin	margen	meteor	meteoro
marine	marino	methodic	metódico
maritime	marítimo	meticulous	meticuloso
mark (n.)	marca	metre	metro
mark (v.)	marcar	metropolis	metrópoli
martyr (n.)	mártir	militarily	militarmente
marvel	maravilla	military	militar
marvellous	maravilloso	militia	milicia
mask	máscara	million	millón
mass	masa	mine (n.)	mina
match (sports)	match	miner	minero
material (adj.)	material	mineral	mineral
maternal	materno	miniature	miniatura
mathematical	matemático	minimum	mínimo
matrimony	matrimonio	ministry	ministro
matron	matrona	minority	minoría
maximum	máximo	minute	minuto
mechanical	mecánico	miserable	miserable
mechanism	mecanismo	misery	miseria
medal	medalla	mission	misión
median	media	mix	mixto
mediate	mediar	mobile	móvil
mediation	meditación	mobilize	movilizar
medicine	medicina	mode	moda
mediocrity	mediocridad	model	modelo
meditate	meditar	moderate (v.)	moderar
melancholic	melancólico	moderation	moderación
melancholy	melancolía	modern	moderno
melody	melodía	modest	modesto
melon	melón	modesty	modestia
member	miembro	modification	modificación
memorable	memorable	modify	modificar
memory	memoria	mould	molde
mental	mental	moment	momento
mentally	mentalmente	momentarily	momentánea-mente
mention (v.)	mencionar		
menu	menú	momentary	momentáneo
mercantile	mercantil	monarch	monarca

monastery	monasterio	mystery	mistério
money	moneda	mystic	místico
monologue	monólogo	mystification	mistificación
monopoly	monopolio		
monosyllable	monosílabo	narrate	narrar
monotonous	monótono	narration	narración
monotony	monotonía	nascent	naciente
monster	monstruo	natal	natal
monstrous	monstruoso	nation	nación
monument	monumento	national	nacional
monumental	monumental	nationality	nacionalidad
moral	moral	native	nativo
moralist	moralista	natural	natural
morality	moralidad	naturally	naturalmente
morbid	morboso	naval	naval
moribund	moribundo	navigable	navegable
mortal	mortal	navigation	navegación
mortify	mortificar	necessarily	necesariamente
motivate	motivar	necessary	necesario
motive	motivo	necessitate	necesitar
motor	motor	necessity	necesidad
mount (n.)	monte	negative	negativo
mountain	montaña	negligence	negligencia
movable	movible	negligent	negligente
move (n.)	mover	negotiation	negociación
movement	movimiento	Negro	negro
multiple	múltiple	nerve	nervio
multiply	multiplicar	nervous	nervioso
multitude	multitud	neutral	neutro
mundane	mundano	no	no
municipal	municipal	noble (adj.)	noble
municipality	municipalidad	nocturnal	nocturno
murmur (n.)	murmurio	nomination	nominación
murmur (v.)	murmurar	normal	normal
muscle	músculo	north	norte
museum	museo	notable	notable
music	música	notary	notario
muslin	muselina	note (n.)	nota
mutilate	mutilar	note (v.)	notar
mutual	mutuo	notice (n.)	noticia
mysterious	misterioso	notify	notificar

notion	noción	omission	omisión
notorious	notorio	omit	omitir
novel (n.)	novela	omnibus	ómnibus
novelist	novelista	omnipotent	omnipotente
nucleus	núcleo	opera	ópera
number	número	operate	operar
nutrition	nutrición	operation	operación
		opinion	opinión
oasis	oasis	opportunity	oportunidad
obedience	obediencia	opposition	oposición
obedient	obediente	oppression	opresión
obelisk	obelisco	optic	óptico
object	objeto	optimism	optimismo
objection	objeción	optimist	optimista
objective	objetivo	opulence	opulencia
obligation	obligación	oracle	oráculo
obligatory	obligatorio	oration	oración
oblige	obligar	orator	orador
oblique	oblicuo	orchestra	orquesta
obscure	obscuro	ordinary	ordinario
obscurity	obscuridad	organic	orgánico
observe	observar	organism	organismo
observer	observador	organization	organización
obstacle	obstáculo	orgy	orgía
obstinacy	obstinación	orifice	orificio
obstruct	obstruir	origin	origen
obtain	obtener	original	original
occasion	ocasión	originality	originalidad
occupation	ocupación	ornament	ornamento
occupy	ocupar (se)	orthography	ortografía
occur	ocurrir	oscillate	oscilar
occurrence	ocurrencia	ostentation	ostentación
ocean	océano	overture	obertura
odious	odioso	oxygen	oxígeno
offend	ofender		
offense	ofensa	pacific	pacífico
offensive	ofensiva	pact	pacto
offer	oferta	pagan	pagano
office	oficio	page	página
officially	oficialmente	palace	palacio
olive	oliva	pallid	pálido

palm	palma	pensive	pensativo
palpitate	palpitar	penumbra	penumbra
panic	pánico	perceptible	perceptible
panorama	panorama	perfect (v.)	perfeccionar
papa	papá	perfection	perfección
paradise	paraíso	perfectly	perfectamente
parallel	paralelo	perfidious	pérfido
paralyse	paralizar	perfume (v.)	perfumar
pardon (n.)	perdón	period	período
pardon (v.)	perdonar	periodic	periódico
parliamentary	parlamentario	permanent	permanente
part	parte	permission	permiso
partial	parcial	permit (n.)	permiso
participate	participar	permit (v.)	permitir
participation	participación	perpetual	perpetuo
particular (adj.)	particular	persecution	persecución
particularly	particularmente	persevere	perseverar
pass (v.)	pasar	persist	persistir
passion	pasión	person	persona
passive	pasivo	personal	personal
past	pasado	personality	personalidad
paste	pasta	personally	personalmente
pastor	pastor	perspective	perspectiva
paternal	paterno	perspicacious	perspicaz
pathetic	patético	persuade	persuadir
patience	paciencia	perturb	perturbar
patio	patio	perverse	perverso
patriarch	patriarca	perversity	perversidad
patriot	patriota	pest	peste
patriotism	patriotismo	petal	pétalo
patron	patrón	petition	petición
pause	pausa	petroleum	petróleo
pavement	pavimento	pharmacy	farmacia
pearl	perla	phenomena	fenómeno
pedagogue	pedagogo	philosopher	filósofo
pedant	pedante	philosophical	filosófico
pedestal	pedestal	philosophy	filosofía
pendulum	péndulo	phosphorus	fósforo
penetrate	penetrar	photograph	fotografía
peninsula	península	photograph (v.)	fotografiar
pension	pensión	phrase	frase

physical	físico	possibility	posibilidad
piano	piano	possible	posible
piety	piedad	postal	postal
pilot	piloto	posterity	posteridad
pine	pino	potency	potencia
pipe	pipa	practical	práctico
pirate	pirata	practically	prácticamente
pistol	pistola	practice (n.)	práctica
placid	plácido	practise (v.)	practicar
plague	plaga	preamble	preámbulo
plan	plan	precaution	precaución
plane	plano	precede	preceder
planet	planeta	precedent	precedente
plant (n.)	planta	precept	precepto
plant (v.)	plantar	precious	precioso
plastic	plástico	precipice	precipicio
plate (n.)	plato	precipitate	precipitar
plate (v.)	platear	precipitation	precipitación
plenitude	plenitud	precisely	precisamente
poem	poema	precision	precisión
poet	poeta	precursor	precursor
poetical	poético	predecessor	predecesor
poetry	poesía	predominance	predominancia
polar	polar	prefect	prefecto
pole	polo	prefecture	prefectura
polemic	polémica	prefer	preferir
police	policía	preferable	preferible
political	político	preference	preferencia
pomp	pompa	prejudiced	prejuicio
pompous	pomposo	prelate	prelado
ponder	ponderar	preliminary	preliminar
popular	popular	premature	prematuro
polularity	popularidad	preoccupation	preocupación
populous	populoso	preoccupied	preocupado
porcelain	porcelana	preparation	preparación
port	puerto	preposition	preposición
portal	portal	prerogative	prerogativa
portion	porción	prescribe	prescribir
position	posición	presence	presencia
positive	positivo	present (v.)	presentar
possession	posesión	presentation	presentación

LIST OF COGNATES
103

presentiment	presentimiento	progress	progreso
preserve	preservar	progressive	progresivo
preside	presidir	progressively	progresivamente
presidency	presidencia	prohibition	prohibición
president	presidente	proletariat	proletario
prestige	prestigio	prologue	prólogo
presume	presumir	prolong	prolongar
pretension	pretensión	promise (n.)	promesa
pretext	pretexto	promptitude	prontitud
prevail	prevalecer	pronounce	pronunciar
prevention	prevención	propaganda	propaganda
prevision	previsión	prophet	profeta
primary	primero	propitious	propicio
primitive	primitivo	proportion	proporción
princess	princesa	proposition	proposición
principal (adj.)	principal	proprietor	propietario
principle (n.)	principio	prosaic	prosaico
prism	prisma	proscribe	proscribir
prison	prisión	prose	prosa
prisoner	prisionero	prosperity	prosperidad
privation	privación	prosperous	próspero
privilege	privilegio	protection	protección
probability	probabilidad	protector	protector
probable	probable	protest (v.)	protestar
probably	probablemente	protestant	protestante
problem	problema	protestation	protestación
proceed	proceder	proverb	proverbio
procession	procesión	providence	providencia
proclaim	proclamar	province	provincia
proclamation	proclamación	provincial	provincial
procure	procurar	provision	provisión
prodigious	prodigioso	provoke	provocar
product	producto	proximity	proximidad
production	producción	prudence	prudencia
profane	profano	prudent	prudente
profession	profesión	psychology	psicología
professional	profesional	public	público
professor	profesor	publication	publicación
profound	profundo	publicity	publicidad
profoundly	profundamente	publish	pubilcar
programme	programa	puerile	pueril

pulpit	púlpito	recommend	recomendar
pulse	pulso	recommenda-	recomendación
pupil (eye)	pupila	tion	
pure	puro	recompense (n.)	recompensa
purely	puramente	recompense (v.)	recompensar
purify	purificar	reconcile	reconciliar
pyramid	pirámide	reconstitute	reconstituir
		reconstruct	reconstruir
quarter	cuarto	recourse	recurso
quiet	quieto	recover	recobrar
quietude	quietud	recreation	recreación
		recruit (v.)	recrutar
race (n.)	raza	rectangle	rectángulo
radiant	radiante	rectify	rectificar
radiator	radiador	rectitude	rectitud
radical	radical	redouble	redoblar
rail	rail	reduce	reducir
ranch	rancho	reduction	reducción
rancour	rencor	re-election	reelección
rapid	rápido	refectory	refectorio
rapidity	rapidez	reference	referencia
rare	raro	refine	refinar
rarely	raramente	refinement	refinamiento
rat	rato	reflect	reflejar
rational	racional	reflexion	reflexión
ray	rayo	reform (n.)	reforma
reaction	reacción	reform (v.)	reformar
realist	realista	refractory	refractario
reality	realidad	refuge	refugio
realization	realización	regale	regalar
reason (n.)	razón	regime	régimen
reason (v.)	razonar	regiment	regimiento
reasonable	razonable	region	región
rebel	rebelde	regular	regular
rebellion	rebelión	regularity	regularidad
receive	recibir	regularly	regularmente
recently	recientemente	regulator	regulador
reception	recepción	reign (v.)	reinar
reciprocal	recíproco	reiterate	reiterar
recite	recitar	rejuvenate	rejuvenecer
recommence	recomenzar	relate	relatar

relation	relación
relative (*adv.*)	relativo
relief (sculpture)	relieve
religion	religión
religious	religioso
remedy	remedio
remedy (*v.*)	remediar
remit	remitir
renounce	renunciar
renovation	renovación
repair (*v.*)	reparar
reparation	reparación
repent	arrepentirse
repose (*v.*)	reposar
repose (*n.*)	reposo
represent	representar
representation	representación
representative	representante
repression	represión
reproach (*n.*)	reproche
reproduce	reproducir
reptile	reptil
republican	republicano
repugnance	repugnancia
reputation	reputación
require	requerir
resentment	resentimiento
reserve (*n.*)	reserva
reserve (*v.*)	reservar
reside	residir
residence	residencia
resignation	resignación
resin	resina
resist	resistir
resistance	resistencia
resolution	resolución
respect (*v.*)	respetar
respectable	respetable
respectful	respetuoso
respective	respectivo

respiration	respiración
respire	respirar
resplendent	resplandeciente
respond	responder
responsibility	responsabilidad
responsible	responsable
rest (remainder)	resto
restore	restaurar
result (*n.*)	resultado
retard	retardar
retire	retirar
return (*v.*)	retornar
reunion	reunión
reunite	reunir
revelation	revelación
reverence	reverencia
revision	revisión
revolt (*n.*)	revuelta
revolt (*v.*)	revoltar
revolutionary	revolucionario
revolve	revolver
rhetoric	retórica
rheumatism	reumatismo
rich	rico
ridiculous	ridículo
rigour	rigor
rigorous	riguroso
rigorously	rigurosamente
rite	rito
rival	rival
robust	robusto
rock	roca
romance	romance
romantic	romántico
rose	rosa
rotund	rotundo
route (*n.*)	ruta
rude	rudo
ruffian	rufián
ruin (*n.*)	ruina
ruin (*v.*)	arruinar

ruinous	ruinoso	security	seguridad
rupture	ruptura	seduce	seducir
rural	rural	seduction	seducción
rustic	rústico	selection	selección
		senate	senado
sacrifice (*n.*)	sacrificio	senator	senador
sacrifice (*v.*)	sacrificar	sensation	sensación
salad	ensalada	sensibility	sensibilidad
salary	salario	sensual	sensual
salient	saliente	sentiment	sentimiento
salmon	salmón	sentimental	sentimental
salute (*v.*)	saludar (greet)	separate (*v.*)	separar
salvation	salvación	separately	separadamente
salvo	salva	separation	separación
sanction	sanción	sepulchre	sepulcro
sanctity	santidad	serene	sereno
sane	sano	serenity	serenidad
sarcasm	sarcasmo	serious	serio
satanical	satánico	sermon	sermón
satire	sátira	serpent	serpiente
satisfaction	satisfacción	serve	servir
satisfactory	satisfactorio	service	servicio
satisfied	satisfecho	servile	servil
scandal	escándalo	session	sesión
scandalize	escandalizar	severe	severo
scandalous	escandaloso	severely	severamente
scene	escena	severity	severidad
sceptic	esceptico	sex	sexo
scientific	científico	sign	signo
scruple	escrúpulo	signification	significación
sculpture (*n.*)	esculptura	signify	significar
season (*v.*)	sazonar	silence	silencio
second	segundo	silent	silencioso
secondary	secundario	silently	silenciosamente
secret (*n.*)	secreto	silhouette	silueta
secret (*adj.*)	secreto	simplicity	simplicidad
secretary	secretaría	simplify	simplificar
secretly	secretamente	simultaneous	simultáneo
sect	secta	simultaneously	simultáneamente
section	sección	sincere	sincero
secular	secular	sincerely	sinceramente

sincerity	sinceridad	stupefaction	estupefacción
singular	singular	stupid	estúpido
singularly	singularmente	stupor	estupor
sinister	siniestro	style	estilo
siren	sirena	suave	suave
situate	situar	subject (*n.*)	sujeto
situation	situación	sublime	sublime
sobriety	sobriedad	submarine	submarino
social	social	submerge	sumergir
socialist	socialista	subordinate (*v.*)	subordinar
solemn	solemne	subscribe	subscribir
solemnity	solemnidad	subsist	subsistir
solicit	solicitar	substance	substancia
solicitude	solicitud	substitute (*n.*)	substituto
solid	sólido	substitute (*v.*)	substituir
solidarity	solidaridad	substitution	substitución
solidly	sólidamente	subterranean	subterraneo
solitary	solitario	subvention	subvención
soluble	soluble	succession	sucesión
solution	solución	successive	sucesivo
sombre	sombrío	successively	sucesivamente
sonorous	sonoro	successor	sucesor
sophism	sofisma	succumb	sucumbir
space	espacio	suffer	sufrir
special	especial	sufficient	suficiente
specially	especialmente	sufficiently	suficientemente
speculation	especulación	suffocate	sofocar
spiral	espiral	suggestion	sugestión
spiritual	espiritual	suicide	suicidio
splendid	espléndido	sum	suma
splendour	esplendor	superficial	superficial
spontaneous	espontáneo	superfluous	superfluo
spontaneously	espontáneamente	superhuman	sobrehumano
station	estación	superintendent	superintendente
statue	estatua	superior (*adv.*)	superior
statute	estatuto	superiority	superioridad
sterile	estéril	supernatural	sobrenatural
stomach	estómago	superstition	superstición
strangle	estrangular	supplementary	suplementario
strictly	estrictamente	supplicant	suplicante
structure	estructura	supply	suplir

support	soportar	terrestrial	terrestre
supposition	suposición	terrible	terrible
suppression	supresión	terribly	terriblemente
supreme	supremo	territory	territorio
surprise (n.)	sorpresa	terror	terror
susceptible	susceptible	testament	testamento
suspend	suspender	testimony	testimonio
suspense	suspenso	text	texto
suspension	suspensión	theatre	teatro
sustain	sustentar	theme	tema
syllable	sílaba	theology	teología
symbol	símbolo	theoretically	teóricamente
syndic	síndico	theory	teoría
syndicate	sindicato	thermometer	termómetro
synthetic	sintético	thesis	tesis
system	sistema	throne	trono
systematic	sistemático	tiger	tigre
		timidity	timidez
taciturn	taciturno	timidly	tímidamente
tact	tacto	tint	tinte
tactics	táctica	tobacco	tabaco
talent	talento	tolerance	tolerancia
tardy	tardo	tolerate	tolerar
tariff	tarifa	tone	tono
technique	técnica	torment (n.)	tormento
telegram	telegrama	torment (v.)	tormentar
telegraph (n.)	telégrafo	torrent	torrente
telegraph (v.)	telegrafiar	torture (n.)	tortura
telephone	teléfono	torture (v.)	torturar
telescope	telescopio	totality	totalidad
temperament	temperamento	totally	totalmente
temperature	temperatura	tourist	turista
tempest	tempestad	tradition	tradición
temple	templo	traditional	tradicional
temporary	temporal	tragedy	tragedia
tendency	tendencia	tragic	trágico
tendon	tendón	train	tren
tension	tensión	tranquil	tranquilo
terminate	terminar	tranquilly	tranquilamente
terrace	terraza	transcendental	transcendental
terrain	terreno	transform	transformar

transformation	transformación	university (*n.*)	universidad
transition	transición	university (*adj.*)	universitario
transmit	transmitir	unjust	injusto
transparent	transparente	unstable	instable
transport (*n.*)	transporte	urbane	urbano
tremulous	trémulo	urgency	urgencia
trespass	traspasar	urgent	urgente
triangle	triángulo	use (*v.*)	usar
tribe	tribu	usual	usual
tribunal	tribunal	usurp	usurpar
tribune	tribuna	usury	usura
tricoloured	tricolor	utility	utilidad
triple	triple	utilization	utilización
triumph (*n.*)	triunfo	utilize	utilizar
triumph (*v.*)	triunfar		
triumphant	triunfante	vacant	vacante
trophy	trofeo	vacation	vacaciones
tropic	trópico	vacillate	vacilar
trot	trotar	vacillation	vacilación
troubadour	trovador	vagabond	vagabundo
trumpeter	trompetero	vague	vago
trunk	tronco	vaguely	vagamente
tube	tubo	valorous	valeroso
tumult	tumulto	valiant	valiente
tunic	túnica	valour	valor
tunnel	túnel	vanguard	vanguardia
turbulent	turbulento	vanity	vanidad
type	tipo	vapour	vapor
typical	típico	variable	variable
tyranny	tiranía	variation	variación
		variety	variedad
ulterior	ulterior	vary	variar
ultimate	último	vassal	vasallo
unanimous	unánime	vast	vasto
unguent (*n.*)	ungüento	vegetable (*adj.*)	vegetal
uniform (*adj.*)	uniforme	vehemence	vehemencia
union	unión	vehicle	vehículo
united	unido	vein	vena
unity	unidad	velocity	velocidad
universal	universal	vendor	vendedor
universe	universo	venerable	venerable

venerate	venerar	violin	violín
veneration	veneración	virgin	virgen
vengeance	venganza	virile	viril
venom	veneno	virility	virilidad
venomous	venenoso	virtue	virtud
verb	verbo	virtuous	virtuoso
verbal	verbal	viscount	vizconde
verdure	verdura	visible	visible
verify	verificar	visibly	visiblemente
verse	verso	vision	visión
version	versión	visit (n.)	visita
vertical	vertical	visit (v.)	visitar
veteran	veterano	visitor	visitador
vibrate	vibrar	vital	vital
vice	vicio	vituperation	vituperio
vicious	vicioso	vivacity	vivacidad
victim	víctima	vocation	vocación
victory	victoria	volcano	volcán
vigil	vigilia	volt	voltio
vigilance	vigilancia	volume	volumen
vigour	vigor	voluntarily	voluntariamente
vigorous	vigoroso	voluntary	voluntario
villain	villano	voluptuous	voluptuoso
vinegar	vinagre	vomit	vomitar
violation	violación	vote (n.)	voto
violence	violencia	vote (v.)	votar
violent	violento	vulgar	vulgar
violently	violentemente		
violet	violeta	zone	zona

A Glossary of Grammatical Terms

E. F. BLEILER

This section is intended to refresh your memory of grammatical terms or to clear up difficulties you may have had in understanding them. Before you work through the grammar you should have a reasonably clear idea what the parts of speech and parts of a sentence are. This is not for reasons of pedantry, but simply because it is easier to talk about grammar if we agree upon terms. Grammatical terminology is as necessary to the study of grammar as the names of automobile parts are to garage men.

This list is not exhaustive, and the definitions do not pretend to be complete, or to settle points of interpretation that grammarians have been disputing for several hundred years. It is a working analysis rather than a scholarly investigation. The definitions given, however, represent most typical American usage, and should serve for basic use.

The Parts of Speech

English words can be divided into eight important groups: nouns, adjectives, articles, verbs, adverbs, pronouns, prepositions and conjunctions. The boundaries between one group of words and another are sometimes vague and ill-felt in English, but a good dictionary can help you make decisions in questionable cases. Always bear in mind, however, that the way a word is used in a sentence may be just as important as the nature of the word itself in deciding what part of speech the word is.

Nouns. *Nouns* are the *words* for *things* of all *sorts*, whether these *things* are real *objects* that you can see, or *ideas*, or *places*, or *qualities*, or *groups*, or more abstract *things*. *Examples* of *words* that are *nouns* are *cat*, *vase*, *door*, *shrub*, *wheat*, *university*, *mercy*, *intelligence*, *ocean*, *plumber*, *pleasure*, *society*, *army*. If you are in *doubt* whether a given *word* is a *noun* try putting the *word* "my" or "this" or "large" (or some other known *adjective*) in *front* of it. If it makes *sense* in the *sentence* the *chances* are that the *word* in *question* is a noun. [All the *words* in *italics* in this *paragraph* are *nouns*.]

Adjectives. Adjectives are the words which describe or give you *specific* information about the *various* nouns in a sentence. They tell you size, colour, weight, pleasantness and many *other* qualities. *Such* words as *big*, *expensive*, *terrible*, *insipid*, *hot*, *delightful*, *ruddy*, *informative* are all *clear* adjectives. If you are in *any* doubt whether a *certain* word is an adjective, add -er to it, or put the word "more" or "too" in front of it. If it makes *good* sense in the sentence, and does not end in -ly, the chances are that it is an adjective. (Pronoun-adjectives will be described under pronouns.) [The adjectives in the *above* sentences are in italics.]

Articles. There are only two kinds of articles in English, and they are easy to remember. The definite article is "the" and the indefinite article is "a" or "an".

Verbs. Verbs *are* the words that *tell* what action, or condition, or relationship *is going* on. Such words as *was*, *is*, *jumps*, *achieved*, *keeps*, *buys*, *sells*, *has finished*, *run*, *will have*, *may*, *should pay*, *indicates are* all verb forms. *Observe* that a verb *can be composed* of more than one word, as *will have* and *should pay*, above; these *are called* compound verbs. As a rough guide for verbs, *try adding* -ed to the word you *are wondering* about, or *taking* off an -ed that *is* already there. If it *makes* sense the chances *are* that it *is* a verb. (This *does* not always *work*, since the so-called strong or irregular verbs *make* forms by *changing* their middle vowels, like *spring, sprang, sprung*.) [Verbs in this paragraph *are* in italics.]

Adverbs. An adverb is a word that supplies additional information about a verb, an adjective or another adverb. It *usually* indicates time, or manner, or place, or degree. It tells you *how*, or *when*, or *where*, or to what degree things are happening. Such words as *now, then, there, not, anywhere, never, somehow, always, very*, and most words ending in *-ly* are *normally* adverbs. [Italicized words are adverbs.]

Pronouns. Pronouns are related to nouns, and take their place. (Some grammars and dictionaries group pronouns and nouns together as substantives.) They mention persons, or objects of any sort without actually giving their names.

There are several different kinds of pronouns. (1) Personal pronouns: by a grammatical convention *I, we, me, mine, us, ours* are called first person pronouns, since *they* refer to the speaker; *you* and *yours* are called second person pronouns, since *they* refer to the person addressed; and *he, him, his, she, her, hers, they, them, theirs* are called third person pronouns, since *they* refer to the things or persons discussed. (2) Demonstrative pronouns: *this, that, these, those.* (3) Interrogative, or question, pronouns: *who, whom, what, whose, which.* (4) Relative pronouns, or pronouns *which* refer back to something already mentioned: *who, whom, that, which.* (5) Others: *some, any, anyone, no one, other, whichever, none,* etc.

Pronouns are difficult for *us,* since our categories are not as clear as in some other languages, and *we* use the same words for *what* foreign-language speakers see as different situations. First, our interrogative and relative pronouns overlap, and must be separated in translation. The easiest way is to observe whether a question is involved in the sentence. Examples: "*Which* [int.] do *you* like?" "The inn, *which* [rel.] was not far from Cadiz, had a restaurant." "*Who* [int.] is there?" "*I* don't know *who* [int.] was there." "The porter *who* [rel.] took our bags was Number 2132." *This* may seem to be a trivial difference to an English speaker, but in some languages *it* is very important.

Secondly, there is an overlap between pronouns and adjectives. In some cases the word "this", for example, is a pronoun; in other cases *it* is an adjective. *This* also holds true for *his, its, her, any, none, other, some, that, these, those,* and many other words. Note whether the word in question stands alone or is associated with another word. Examples: "*This* [pronoun] is mine." "This [adj.] taxi has no springs." Watch out for the word "that", which can be a pronoun or an adjective or a conjunction. And remember that "my", "your", "our" and "their" are always adjectives. [All pronouns in this section are in italics.]

Prepositions. Prepositions are the little words that introduce phrases that tell *about* condition, time, place, manner, association, degree and similar topics. Such words as *with, in, beside, under, of, to, about, for* and *upon* are prepositions. *In* English prepositions and adverbs overlap, but, as you will see *by* checking *in* your dictionary, there are usually differences *of* meaning *between* the two uses. [Prepositions *in* this paragraph are designated *by* italics.]

Conjunctions. Conjunctions are joining-words. They enable you to link words *or* groups of words into larger units, *and* to build compound *or* complex sentences out of simple sentence units. Such words as *and, but, although, or, unless* are typical conjunctions. *Although* most conjunctions are easy enough to identify, the word "that" should be watched closely to see *that* it is not a pronoun *or* an adjective. [Conjunctions italicized.]

Words about Verbs

Verbs are responsible for most of the terminology in this short grammar. The basic terms are:

Conjugation. In many languages verbs fall into natural groups, according to the way they make their forms. These groupings are called conjugations, and are an aid to learning grammatical structure. Though it may seem difficult at first to speak of First and Second Conjugations, these are simply short ways of saying that verbs belonging to these classes make their forms according to certain consistent rules, which you can memorize.

Infinitive. This is the basic form which most dictionaries give for verbs in most languages, and in most languages it serves as the basis for classifying verbs. In English (with a very few exceptions) it has no special form. To find the infinitive for any English verb, just fill in this sentence: "I like to . . . (walk, run, jump, swim, carry, disappear, etc.")". The infinitive in English is usually preceded by the word "to".

Tense. This is simply a formal way of saying "time". In English we think of time as being broken into three great segments: past, present and future. Our verbs are assigned forms to indicate this division, and are further subdivided for shades of meaning. We subdivide the present time into the present (I walk) and present progressive (I am walking); the past into the simple past (I walked), progressive past (I was walking), perfect or present perfect (I have walked), past perfect or pluperfect (I had walked); and future into simple future (I shall walk) and future progressive (I shall be walking). These are the most common English tenses.

Present Participles, Progressive Tenses. In English the present participle always ends in -ing. It can be used as a noun or an adjective in some situations, but its chief use is in *forming* the so-called progressive tenses. These are made by *putting* appropriate forms of the verb "to be" before a present participle: In "to walk" [an infinitive], for example, the present progressive would be: I am *walking*, you are *walking*, he is *walking*, etc.; past progressive, I was *walking*, you were *walking* and so on. [Present participles are in italics.]

Past Participles, Perfect Tenses. The past participle in English is not *formed* as regularly as is the present participle. Sometimes it is *constructed* by adding -ed or -d to the present tense, as *walked, jumped, looked, received*; but there are many verbs where it is *formed* less regularly: *seen, been, swum, chosen, brought*. To find it, simply fill out the sentence "I have . . ." putting in the verb form that your ear tells you is right for the particular verb. If you speak grammatically you will have the past participle.

Past participles are sometimes used as adjectives: "Don't cry over *spilt* milk." Their most important use, however, is to form the system of verb tenses that are *called* the perfect tenses: present perfect (or perfect), past perfect (or pluperfect), etc. In English the present perfect tense is *formed* with the present tense of "to have" and the past participle of a verb: I have *walked*, you have *run*, he has *begun*, etc. The past perfect is *formed*, similarly, with the past tense of "to have" and the past participle: I had *walked*, you had *run*, he had *begun*. Most of the languages you are likely to study have similar systems of perfect tenses, though they may not be *formed* in exactly the same way as in English. [Past participles in italics.]

Preterite, Imperfect. Many languages have more than one verb tense for expressing an action that took place in the past. They may use a perfect tense (which we have just covered), or a preterite, or an imperfect. English, although you may never have thought about it, is one of these languages, for we can say "I have spoken to him" [present perfect], or "I spoke to him" [simple past], or "I was speaking to him" [past progressive]. These sentences do not mean exactly the same thing, although the differences are subtle, and are difficult to put into other words.

While usage differs a little from language to language, if a language has both a preterite and an imperfect, in general the preterite corresponds to the English simple past (I ran, I swam, I spoke), and the imperfect corresponds to the English past progressive (I was running, I was swimming, I was speaking). If you are curious to discover the mode of thought behind these different tenses, try looking at the situation in terms of background-action and point-action. One of the most important uses of the imperfect is to provide a background against which a single point-action can take place. For example, "When I was walking down the street [background, continued over a period of time, hence past progressive or imperfect], I stubbed my toe [an instant or point of time, hence a simple past or preterite]."

Reflexive. This term, which sounds more difficult than it really is, simply means that the verb refers back to the noun or pronoun that is its subject. In modern English the reflexive pronoun always ends with -self, and we do not use the construction very frequently. In other languages, however, reflexive forms may be used more frequently, and in ways that do not seem very logical to an English speaker. Examples of English reflexive sentences: "He washes himself." "He seated himself at the table."

Passive. In some languages, like Latin, there is a strong feeling that an action or thing that is taking place can be expressed in two different ways. One can say, A does-something-to B, which is "active"; or B is-having-something-done-to-him by A, which is "passive". We do not have a strong feeling for this classification of experience in English, but the following examples should indicate the difference between an active and a passive verb: Active: "John is building a house." Passive: "A house is being built by John." Active: "The steamer carried the cotton to England." Passive: "The cotton was carried by the steamer to England." Bear in mind that the formation of passive verbs and the situations where they can be used vary enormously from language to language. This is one situation where you usually cannot translate English word for word into another language and make sense.

Miscellaneous Terms

Comparative, Superlative. These two terms are used with adjectives and adverbs. They indicate the degree of strength within the meaning of the word. Faster, better, earlier, newer, more rapid, more detailed, more suitable are examples of the comparative in adjectives, while more rapidly, more recently, more suitably are comparatives for adverbs. In most cases, as you have seen, the comparative uses -er or "more" for an adjective, and "more" for an adverb. Superlatives are those forms which end in -est or have "most" prefixed before them for adjectives, and "most" prefixed for adverbs: most intelligent, earliest, most rapidly, most suitably.

Gender. Gender should not be confused with actual sex. In many languages nouns are arbitrarily assigned a gender (masculine or feminine, or masculine or feminine or neuter), and this need not correspond to sex. You simply have to learn the pattern of the language you are studying in order to become familiar with its use of gender.

Idiom. An idiom is an expression that is peculiar to a language, the meaning of which is not the same as the literal meaning of the individual words composing it. Idioms, as a rule, cannot be translated word by word into another language. Examples of English idioms: *"Take it easy."* "Don't *beat about the bush.*" "It *turned out* to be *a Dutch treat.*" "Can you *tell the time* in Spanish?"

The Parts of the Sentence

Subject, Predicate. In grammar *every complete sentence* contains two basic parts, the subject and the predicate. *The subject*, if *we* state the terms most simply, is the thing, person, or activity talked about. *It* can be a noun, a pronoun or something *that* serves as a noun. *A subject* would include, in a typical case, a noun, the articles or adjectives *which* are associated with it and perhaps phrases. Note that in complex sentences *each part* may have its own subject. [*The subjects of the sentences above* have been italicized.]

The predicate *talks about the subject.* In a formal sentence the predicate *includes a verb, its adverbs, predicate adjectives, phrases and objects*—whatever *happens to be present.* A predicate adjective *is an adjective* which *happens to be in the predicate after a form of the verb to be.* Example: "Apples *are red.*" [Predicates *are in italics.*]

In the following simple sentences subjects are in italics, predicates in italics and underlined. "*Green apples are bad for your digestion.*" "When *I go to Spain, I always stop in Cadiz.*" "*The man with the suitcase is travelling to Madrid.*"

Direct and Indirect Objects. Some verbs (called transitive verbs) take direct and/or indirect objects in their predicates; other verbs (called intransitive verbs) do not take objects of any sort. In English, except for pronouns, objects do not have any special forms, but in languages which have case forms or more pronoun forms than English, objects can be troublesome.

The direct object is the person, thing, quality or matter that the verb directs *its action* upon. It can be a pronoun, or a noun, perhaps accompanied by an article and/or adjectives. The direct object always directly follows *its verb,* except when there is also an indirect object pronoun present, which comes between the verb and the object. Prepositions do not go before direct objects. Examples: "The cook threw *green onions* into the stew." "The border guards will want to see *your passport* tomorrow." "Give *it* to me." "Please give me *a glass of red wine.*" [We have placed *direct objects* in this paragraph in italics.]

The indirect object, as grammars will tell *you,* is the person or thing for or to whom the action is taking place.

It can be a pronoun or a noun with or without article and adjectives. In most cases the words "to" or "for" can be inserted before it, if not already there. Examples: "Please tell *me* the time." "I wrote *her* a letter from Barcelona." "We sent *Mr. Gonzalez* ten pesos." "We gave *the most energetic guide* a large tip." [Indirect objects are in italics.]

Index

The following abbreviations have been used in this index; *adj.* for adjective, *conj.* for conjugation, *def.* for definition, *prep.* for preposition, *pron.* for pronoun and *vb.* for verb. Spanish words appear in *italics* and their English translations in parentheses.